From
Bollington
to Zanzibar

Execution Stone, Swaziland

Graham Hibbert

These memories are dedicated to my wife Elsie,
my children Jane and Peter
and my grandchildren Christopher and Samuel.

ACKNOWLEDGMENTS

I wish to thank the following people all of whom I have had the privilege to meet and who have enriched my life. Few of them will remember me but I will certainly remember them. They are not listed in any special order and they are not necessarily featured in my memories here:

Dusty Springfield, Felicity Goodie, Anita Roddick, Stuart Hall, His Excellency President Amani Karume, Sheikh Al Sayed, Abdul Khaliq Al-Abed, the Duke and Duchess of Gloucester, the Duke and Duchess of Kent, the Right Hon David Owen, Danny Glover, Keith Barlow, Chief Emeka Anyoukou, Terry Waite, Jimmy Saville, Peter Snow, Sir Trevor McDonald, HRH Sultan of Bahrain, HRH Duke of York, HRH Duke of Edinburgh and Her Majesty the Queen.

CHURNET VALLEY BOOKS
1 King Street, Leek, Staffordshire ST13 5NW 01538 399033
www.leekbooks.co.uk
© Graham Hibbert and Churnet Valley Books 2006
ISBN 1 904546 42 0
(978 1 904546 42 9)

INTRODUCTION

I have had an interesting and sometimes exciting career that took me all over the world and during which I was privileged to meet a number of famous people. The first celebrity I met was before this story begins, when at the age of nine I was paid half a crown (2/6) to ride a scooter down Bowden Street in Macclesfield while a very young Sir John Mills cycled past during the making of the film 'So Well Remembered'.

When I became a fireman it was Elsie and the children who would be left at home, or in the recreation ground, church, pub or in the car just as we were about to go out, as I responded to my fire service bleeper. I would disappear for ten minutes or all day. Elsie was left alone to worry - something that I did not appreciate at the time.

When other families would plan a day out or a school event I would have to make excuses. Sometimes during the day I would be grumpy or I would have to go to bed having been up all night on a fire call.

Later when I was away overseas Elsie would be left on her own again, but later she would travel with me, both in the UK and at overseas business events. These included memorable St John's Ambulance 'blessings' at both of the Liverpool cathedrals and at Hereford cathedral, a wedding in Hong Kong, and what is Elsie's most treasured memory, a meeting with Her Majesty the Queen at Balmoral Castle.

Without Elsie's love and support, I would never have been able to lead such an extra-ordinary life.

Ninety-nine percent of the events in this book are true and are told as best as I remember them, although I can not guarantee that all the locations and names are correctly spelt.

Graham Hibbert 2006

1950s

COME DANCING....

     OR GO SOLDIERING

The glamorous Rhoda Dawson, whose dance salon put Bollington on the map in the 1950s.

CHAPTER I
CONSCRIPTION

Although I was not aware of it at the time, one the most sought-after postings in the British army was the trooping pool based at Netley Hospital, Southampton. This provided the permanent military staff to the chartered troopships that operated out of Southampton and Harwich. The chances of such a posting was by today's standards equivalent to winning the lottery.

THE MEDICAL

Young factory apprentices in the 1950s had four priorities; dancing, sex, how to fail the National Service entrance medical and obtaining the City and Guilds certificate - but not necessarily in that order. How to avoid National Service was always first on the list and sex for the most part, in those days, was just wishful thinking.

It wasn't the thought that you could be sent to a terrorist war area, like Malaya or Cyprus, Aden or Northern Ireland, although it is often forgotten that many national servicemen lost their lives on active service. No, it was the thought of leaving a cosy and pleasant home life for the army at £3 a week, just when you had come onto full pay of £25 a week with overtime.

Dancing dominated life outside work with bands like those of Eric Delaney, Ivy Benson and Johnny Dankworth - with a young singer called Cleo Lane. 'Big bands' often performed within reach of Macclesfield on a Saturday night. Favourite venues were the Sale Locarno, Trentham Gardens and the Buxton Pavilion, with entry for the top bands at around three shillings and sixpence (3/6). We would think nothing of making the four hour journey to Blackpool on a Saturday night (no M6 then) to dance in the Tower Ballroom.

Closer to home we had the Ell Rio club in Macclesfield where I saw the Beatles for two shillings; Ma Eaton's and the Regal Ballroom Alderley Edge, where I met my wife, were also local favourites. In Bollington we had something very special, Rhoda Dawson's, where we spent many happy hours. Rhoda's had one of the finest dance floors in the north of England and was busy seven nights a week. Bollington was so popular on a Friday and Saturday nights in the 50s and 60s that extra late night buses were laid on.

The late fifties and early sixties were a wonderful time to be young, it was the age of stockings, suspenders, mini skirts, rock and roll and the Mini, drugs were virtually unheard of, we drank Watney's Red Barrel (it was awful) and teenagers actually paid for dancing lessons. The English language had yet to be contaminated by American slang, to be gay was to be happy, a 'good screw' was made of brass by GKN Nettlefold and photographs in adult magazines had all the interesting bits blanked out!

Dancing was the key to getting girls. The questions 'do you come here often', 'can I see you home' (with the hope that they did not live 5 miles away!) and, when there was a bar, 'would you like a drink' (first checking that you had 2 shillings and 9 pence and 'other items' in case a brandy and Babycham was indicated) would be asked many times during a dance. The most popular girls' drink was Cherry B, often referred to as 'the virgin's lament'.

Over-shadowing our enjoyment was the thought that only a short time away was two years national service. The only hope to continue this wonderful life was to fail the medical. Factory floor apprentices held meetings to compare notes on how to fail your medical. Without going to extreme measures like pretending to be mental (many tried this), there was flat feet, colour blindness, producing urine the colour of canal water and the learning to stop one's testicles travelling up into your stomach by a special kind of coughing. All were rumoured to be ways to achieve the desired result.

The dreaded day arrived and it was time to put all those theories into practice. The previous day copious quantities of beetroot had been consumed with the aim of 'passing blood', we practised walking flat-footed, incorrectly reading an eye test chart and standing naked in front of a mirror coughing to see if any movement in the scrotum could be detected. Various tablets were dropped into our urine to see which one had the desired 'clouding' effect.

The day of the medical was bitterly cold with a severe frost as hundreds of young men arrived at the damp and unwelcoming Ducie Street clinic in Manchester. First we were documented, the slightest hesitation when asked 'religion' meant you were documented C of E. You were then asked what regiment or corps you would like to serve in; being an auto-electrician in the ambulance building industry I opted for the Royal Electrical & Mechanical Engineers (REME). Some optimistic 'posh' types even asked for the RAF.and the few that opted for the Navy generally spoke in high-pitched voices and walked as if clutching a banana in their buttocks.

The eye test immediately followed our documentation and was carried out by a lowly RASC lance-corporal. You were told to read from a very dirty chart on the wall, starting from the top. I thought I had not better make things too obvious, and I decided I would start to make the deliberate mistakes on line five. 'A', 'DL'. 'Next' the lance corporal shouted, 'hang on I haven't finished yet', I muttered. 'Next.' So much for failing the eye test.

The humiliation then started, we were herded into a large room, split into groups of twenty and told to strip naked, leaving us with nowhere to conceal our soluble aspirin tablets to contaminate our urine samples. We were then taken in batches of about twenty to a series of side rooms, each with one or more doctors waiting to carry out various perverse procedures.

All aspects of the medical seemed to concentrate on orifices, our ears, throats, nostrils and rectums were all examined in great detail, I cannot recollect the use of a blood pressure machine or stethoscope. It was a bitterly cold November day and the MOD were obviously short of coke as the few iron radiators were stone cold (or was this intentional?), the red tiled floor was ice cold, so walking 'flat footed' was out of the question. Another plan bit the dust.

Great importance seemed to involve the urine sample, twenty at a time and still naked we were issued by a man in a brown slop with a yellow stained glass tube and instructed to produce three inches, 'no more no less' - not an easy task when in full flow. 'What, from here,' one berk shouted. Those that could not produce a drop even though they were bursting, would under the supervision of the USC (urine sample collector), better known as 'pissing Willy', go to the washbasins and turn all the taps on in the hope of inducement. It was at this point that young men for the first time would discover true comradeship when those with full bladders provided samples for those less fortunate; the USC seemed to find this practice perfectly acceptable.

There was a bit of paper stuck on each tube with a number on it, the idea being to record the number against your name, but by the time the tubes were wet with their contents the ink had run making the numbers eligible, and the whole process was a farce. I don't believe anyone ever failed a urine test!

The final part of the medical involved a doctor who had an unhealthy interest in the body's dangling parts. I joined the queue to the mortifying news of 'it's a woman', and the queue fell silent as young men concentrated on self control. The RAMC lady doctor, who I remember had a face 'like a dried cow patch', examined every scrotum in great detail, first the left testicle was weighed carefully in the palm of the hand, then the right, then both together, at this point you were instructed to 'cough' - all thoughts of the weak shallow coughing that we had been practising for weeks vanished and great hearty coughs were rendered by all.

Finally we got dressed and retired to nearby pubs to discuss our ordeal and wonder if we would ever meet again. Three weeks later on a cold November morning in 1957 an OHMS brown envelope arrived containing a one way railway docket, instructions to report to the Royal Army Medical Corps (RAMC) training camp at Fleet in Hampshire and an order to take a sheet of brown paper and string, for the return of your civilian clothing.

Of the three Lomas apprentices that had their medical that day, John Gosling, a fully trained panel beater, was posted to the tank corps, myself an electrician was sentenced to the medical corps and Geoffrey Coleman, an amateur footballer, who had absolutely nothing wrong with him came out the best, he failed the medical. Why we were asked what regiment or corps we would like, will forever remain a mystery.

It was a month past my 21st birthday when I finished work at Herbert Lomas to join the army. I wondered if I would have a job to return to after national service, it was the practice in the 1950s to sack apprentices at the age of 21 - companies argued so that they would seek employment with other companies and become more experienced, but in practice it was because we had now come on to full pay.

My 'going in' stag night was held at The Highwayman pub at Rainow, where I got completely 'rat-arsed' and drove home down the steep Blaze Hill in my three cylinder Jowitt van with its OWO (one wheel only) cable breaks, I missed the wall of the Masonic Arms by inches. Very foolish days!

My father took me to Hibel Road station to catch the midnight train to Euston; from there I took the Northern line to Waterloo for the Southern Region connection to Fleet. All over the country hundreds of other young men were embarking on similar journeys to military camps, all no doubt wondering like me, what was in store for them during the next two years? Some of these national servicemen men would see military action against terrorists in Cyprus and Malaya, and some would lose their lives as had many before them.

CHAPTER II
FLEET

Apprehensive, tired and bleary eyed, teens of young men alighted from smoky railway carriages at Fleet station, many had worried all the way that they would not make the midday arrival deadline. Most had travelled overnight; two from the Outer Hebrides had been travelling for two days. Waiting on the station forecourt was a RAMC sergeant and several corporals, all with shining boots and evil faces, and with them were a number of 5 ton trucks with RASC (Royal Army Service Corps) drivers.

We were lined up to be addressed by the sergeant. 'Good morning gentlemen, this is the last time for the next two years you will asked do to anything, in future you will be told, and you will always respond at the double, without question or hesitation. For the next twelve weeks you are sproggs; sproggs are the lowest form of life on earth.'

His voice had started off pleasant and friendly but as he went on it steadily increased in volume and ferocity. 'Now get rid of that camel shit, smoking is bad for you and fag ends make for an untidy camp.' Turf, Pasha, Park Drive and Woodbine fag ends including mine were hastily discarded - and I have never smoked since.

We climbed into the 5 tonners for the ride to the camp; as we passed along the affluent Fleet High Street there were soldiers everywhere, many shouting words of encouragement such as 'get some in', 'you poor bastards', 'only 729 days to do'. We eventually arrived at the camp where the NCOs reported to the guard room (sergeants, corporals, and lance corporals are Non-Commissioned Officers).

Thursday afternoon and Friday was devoted to documentation, kit issue, commanding officer's lecture and padre's lecture, but first we were taken to the mess (dinning room) for a reasonable meal of mince meat, cabbage and mashed potatoes.

Next stop was the regimental office, there you were allocated a squad and a billet, and it was at this point you literally became a number and the process of dehumanisation began, 23435450 Private Hibbert G.G. hut 4, F spider; squad OIC is Corporal Nolan. It turned out that as bastards go

Corporal Nolan wasn't too bad. You wrote your number on the back of your hand and repeated it over and over until it was imprinted in your brain. There are some things in life that you never forget; your army number and the regimental motto, 'In Arduis Fidelis' (Faithful in Adversity). I can guarantee that most national service men can still remember their number

On the parade ground facing the regimental office the NCOs gathered their respective charges and attempted to line them up and 'march' them to their allocated barrack rooms. During the next twelve weeks we would come to hate this parade ground (the square) as we spent many hours 'square bashing'. There were squads of soldiers everywhere, running, marching or walking 'at the double' and all being shouted at by NCOs. Some had a wry smile on their faces as they realised that with the arrival of a new intake they were no longer bottom of the sprogg ladder, they had some other poor sods to look down on and to say the national serviceman's favourite words - 'get some in'. Only three little words but of enormous psychological importance, representing a glimmer of light at the end of a very long tunnel.

On arrival at our billet we each claimed a metal framed bed, and thanks to a friend from my home village, Melvin Davis (now Rev'd Davis), who was a permanent staff clerk at Fleet, I had been tipped off and grabbed a bed close but not too close to the cast iron stove situated in the middle of the room.

Leaving our few civilian belongings next to our bed we collected a mattress from the bedding store along with 2 blankets, woollen, 2 sheets, cotton, 1 pillow and 1 pillow case, cotton, all duly signed for. Again following inside information I tried to avoid a soiled mattress and blankets and sheets with holes, as these would result in 'barrack room damage' stoppages from your measly pay, even though you were not responsible.

We were given five minutes to make our beds, and as most blokes had never made a bed in their lives what a mess most of them were; we would soon to learn the hard way how to make hospital corners and blanket boxes!

Next stop was the uniform store, a form had to be filled in giving chest, arm, leg and head size, and for those you did not know their sizes the camp tailor would give you a cursory glance and fill in the relevant details. It was too much for the army to realise that the tailor, a civilian who was paid to make the necessary alterations to the uniforms, had a vested interest in getting it wrong. Need I say more!

Bags kit 1:

Jacket battledress 1

Trousers battledress 1

Coat great khaki 1

Jacket fatigue 1

Trousers fatigue 1

Belt webbing 1

Gaiters pair 1

Boots pairs 1

Pumps P.T. pairs 1

Shorts P.T. pairs 1

Pants cellular 2

Shirts khaki 2

Socks pairs 2

Berets 2

Badge cap 1

Housewife 1

Tins mess, knife, fork, spoon and mugs enamel one.

Back pack 1

Small gear 1

Epaulets training 2

Other items of kit were issued at later stages of training; ties and lanyards were issued at the end of training because these could be used for the not uncommon suicide attempts. It was pointless because bootlaces were invariably used.

After dumping our kit in wooden lockers at the side of the bed we were marched to the NAAFI shop for the compulsory 'purchase' of Brasso, Blanko, Cherry Blossom black boot polish, two yellow dusters, two sheets brown paper, two shoe brushes, nail brush (for blankoing) a candle and an electric iron between each barrack room. (During the course of training further irons were purchased by individuals or groups). All of these items would be paid for by later deductions on our first pay parade.

By now it was late afternoon on our first day, and I was to learn a salutary lesson - never to volunteer. As our corporal, whose room was at the end of the barrack room, entered, we all jumped to attention. Jumping to attention applied to any NCO or officer who entered the barrack room. 'Would all those who can drive step forward'. I along with several others eagerly moved forward. 'Right you two drive the floor polisher, you two go to the coke compound and get a wheel barrow full of coke, and lock it in the outside bin, take two men and pick-axe handles with you as escort in case of hijack on the way back - (coke was a much sort after commodity) -and do not be tempted to sell not even one piece'.

He continued, 'You will not attempt to light the stove (it was freezing) until I say so, that is a luxury that has to be earned. The rest can go for tea. There will be a four hour bull session at 1800 hours.'

Corporal Nolan stayed with us all evening showing us how to iron trousers, shirts, and battle dress using the brown paper. Creases had to be in exactly the right place but it would take us many weeks to obtain the much prized razor sharp edges. The candles purchased at the NAAFI were not as we assumed in case of power failure but to heat the back of our spoons which were then used to smooth out the dimples on the toe caps of our boots prior to hours of spit and Cherry Blossom applied in tiny circles to achieve a mirror surface.

'Lights out 2200 hours' shouted the corporal. 'There will be no sobbing for Mummy, no playing with your old man, no farting and no going AWOL (absent without leave), anyone attempting to leave this camp without a pass will be caught and sent to Colchester'.(the military prison). There was some sobbing that first night and thanks to the meal of mince with onions and cabbage, farting was loud and continuous. With no windows open due to the severe frost the atmosphere was most unpleasant, and with all these night time noises, in spite of being 'dog' tired, I could not sleep.

Before lights out our corporal informed us, 'The fire siren will sound sometime during the night, this happens once a week, you will have 30 seconds to line up outside at the back of the barrack room. This will be the only time you ever use the rear exit. I will take a roll call, in the event of me not being available the nerk in the first bed who for the time being will be barrack room leader will take the roll call.'

Fire drills were always during the night usually when it was snowing or lashing it down. Later in training we took little notice of the fire siren, until one night I looked out of the window to see flames shooting above the roof tops. We all trooped outside to see with great delight that the tailor's shop was ablaze. The camp Green Goddess arrived and what a shambles it was - it wasn't until the retained fire engine arrived from Fleet that fire fighting got under way.

At 05.30 hours next morning, Bang! Bang! on the bed rails, 'Come on you horrible shower, hands off cocks, hands on socks, move it, move it, breakfast 0630, anyone missing breakfast will be charged, 0730 at the barber's shop for a haircut.' 'I don't need a haircut.' 'Which fairy said that?' 'Me' 'Me what!' 'Me corporal'. 'You great lump of jelly is your head hurting?' 'No corporal.' 'Well it should be, I'm stood on your hair - you will get it cut and report for two hours kitchen fatigues at 1800 hours'.

Smallpox, typhoid, paratyphoid, tetanus, yellow fever, meningitis, hepatitis A & B, polio, and swine fever, you had an injection or vaccination every few days. The most unpleasant was typhoid (TAB) which was always given on Friday afternoons to allow the weekend to recover, the reactions could be very unpleasant with severe pain around the injection, a high temperature and aching limbs. Those not too badly effected brought mugs of tea and food from the mess for those who could not get out of bed. One important vaccination that could determine your posting was the Mantoux test to determine if you had naturally immunity to tuberculosis; my reaction was positive which meant I could safely come into contact with TB patients.

The Medical Officer's (MO) lecture on sex was of particular interest as many of us were at the sharp end of the Ministry of Defences fight against venereal deceases. After seeing photographs of the effects of syphilis and gonorrhoea we came out of that lecture convinced that if we ever kissed a girl again our 'old man' would drop off and we all made a solemn vow never to have sex!

National Servicemen were paid a pittance. I remember my first pay parade lining up in front of a RAPC (Royal Army Pay Corps) Sergeant smartly saluting and holding out your hand to receive two pounds, eight shillings and six pence. You then moved to a table to sign your pay book, the pay was less NAAFI shop payment 4 shillings 8 pence, electric iron fund 2/6d, barrack room damages 2/6d, corporal's fund 6 pence, Padre's welfare fund 1 shilling, hair cut 1/3d, postage home for return of civilian cloths 2 shillings, etc. No one ever queried the amount. Some of these regular stoppages, particularly barrack room damages that appeared every week, were well-managed 'fiddles'. Amongst these stoppages the one minute twice weekly haircut had to be paid for, price 1/3d.

Part One orders were posted on the barrack wall daily, and in addition to routine information these gave details of who was on guard duties, coke compound picket, and frost picket. Personnel for these duties were nominated by the NCOs as a result of shoddy kit, slightly less than immaculate kit - boots, sloppy drill, last out of the shower, back marker on a route march - and the favourite, a blanket box slightly out of line - or just bad luck.

The most sole-destroying picket was frost picket; to prevent pipes freezing every toilet in the spider had to be flushed hourly during the night, all the sink and bath taps run for five minutes each hour, and most important of all Corporal Nolan had to be taken a mug of hot tea at 0545Hrs. Like guard duties and coke compound guard, all these duties meant lack of sleep and you still had to be on parade immaculately polished at 0730 Hrs.

The weekly Part Two orders were much more exciting for these gave details of the passing out parades for the lucky squads at the end of their basic training. Postings were listed, and we used to stand looking in awe and wonder thinking if we would ever reach this stage, posting to Hong Kong, Cyprus, Mauritius, Malta, Gibraltar, Singapore, Aden, Kenya and even attachments in Australia were among many postings in the then very large British Empire. You could be very unlucky and be posted to Aldershot or attached to a Guards or Scottish regiment. The most unpopular posting was Germany. but for a very lucky few there was the trooping pool based at Netley hospital Southampton. Part Two orders also gave details of punishment awarded to those charged and placed on Commanding Officers orders, and those poor souls that had been 'back squaded'.

With the promise of extra pay a few opted to volunteer to go to the chemical warfare research establishment at Porton Down for research into the common cold or for undisclosed special duties on Christmas Island (only now do we partly know the truth about both of these, Porton Down was germ warfare research and Christmas Island was nuclear bomb testing).

Normally there was no leave for twelve weeks, the only exception being Christmas, and our intake was lucky after six weeks. The English, we were allowed home for three days Christmas leave, and the Scots, three days for Hogmonay. There were strict instructions that you were to wear uniform at all times when on leave but little notice was taken of this. It was wonderful to wear shoes and civilian clothes for a few days.

A lot has been written about national service life so I will skip the next ten weeks except to say it consisted of lots of bull, lots of drill, PT, firearms training, as well as classroom training and even education for the less literate.

Many local civilians worked at the camp, many of them on 'perks' from the squaddies. The best paid civilian was undoubtedly the boiler man; his job was to stoke the boilers that supplied each spider with hot water. There were six billets to a spider each sharing a common toilet and bath block, the boiler man looked after six spiders, with squaddies paying 3d a week to a so called coke supplement fund. It meant, even after the billet OIC's 'commission' the boiler man was getting a 'back hander' far in excess of his wage. There were no radiators in the billets - but we always had hot water.

Meals were supplemented in an evening between bull sessions at the NAAFI, where you could get the best double egg and chips in the world. But you could not get 'a drink' - alcohol was only served in the permanent staff messes.

After 4 weeks, if our kit, barrack room and drill passed CO's inspection we were allowed out of camp in uniform for 4 hours on Saturday nights. Throughout the UK dance halls in the vicinity of military establishments were famous for their 'grab a granny' nights; they would attract all the 'loose' women for miles around. For some the temptation was too great, after a few pints, the lectures on the dangers of sex and solemn vows of abstinence were suddenly forgotten. Unlike overseas postings, free from infection kits were not issued in the UK, and many would regret the 'grab a granny' nights.

At last after weeks of rehearsing the passing out day arrived, we proudly marched with the RAMC regimental band. My squad did our very best to win the best squad award; at least we did not come last. The best recruit collected his cup and promptly had to hand it back ready for the next intake. After the parade details of postings were given, we eagerly crowded around the notice board, all the exciting overseas postings were listed, and there were both whoops of delight and groans. That night we all went into Fleet for a 'knees up' and even had a 'whip round' for Corporal Nolan.

'23435450 Private Hibbert G.G. to report to BMH (British Military Hospital) Netley Southampton' was on part 11 orders, Netley hospital specialised in mental disorders and sexual diseases, and the allocation of permanent medical staff for troop ships. But not for me the trooping pool, my posting was as an NO (nursing orderly) an unexciting and boring job. I was disappointed but fate was to intervene.

I packed my kit bag and along with the rest of the squad was taken to Fleet station, where I said goodbye to the many friends I'd made during training and in my now immaculate uniform set off home for one weeks posting leave.

Royal Victoria Hospital, Netley in 1957.

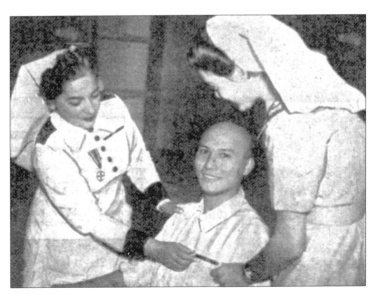

Queen Alexander's nurses have been at the heart of
the Army medical services for a hundred years.

CHAPTER III
NETLEY

The weeks posting leave was pure liberation, wearing civilian clothes for the first time in nearly 4 months was a wonderful feeling. Meeting my friends again, dancing at Rhoda Dawson's, all made the week pass very quickly. After twelve weeks wearing army boots, getting used to shoes again proved difficult and on the last day of leave I badly injured my right ankle.

Within a very short time my foot doubled in size, turned dark blue and was excruciatingly painful. All sorts of fears ran through my mind as my father took me to Macclesfield Infirmary (where Sainsbury's is now), 'Have I broken my ankle?' 'How will I get to Netley?' 'What will happen to me when I get there? and 'Will I be charged with self-inflicted injuries?'

After a short wait in the casualty department I was seen by the infamous Dr. Pickard. Dr Pickard better known as 'the butcher' was a local legend, he was unorthodox but a good casualty doctor who seemed to be on duty for 24 hours a day, 7 days a week. He was well-known for his fast suturing and limb setting without anaesthetics, and he always had a cigarette hanging from the corner of his mouth, even when examining patients.

Dr Pickard entered the cubicle, complete with cigarette, and he twisted my ankle until I howled with pain, declared it was not broken and instructed the nurse to strap it up before moving on to the next unfortunate casualty. (In all fairness while Dr Pickard was perhaps a little eccentric he was highly respected and many Macclesfield people owe their lives to him.)

Next morning my father again took me to Hibel Road Station along with all my kit, and as I would not be able to manage the underground he gave me money for a taxi from Euston to Waterloo from where I would get the Southern Region Southampton train. On arrival at Southampton I took the local Portsmouth train to Netley.

I must have looked a sorry sight on Netley station wearing one boot and one pump, hopping along the platform dragging my kit bag. Two chaps in civilian clothes approached 'Are you posted or a patient?' they asked. 'Both' I replied. 'Hang on here mate and we will send a truck for you'. This was music to my ears - and to be called 'mate' as well. Twenty minutes later a

Bedford 3 ton truck arrived, I was hauled into the back and welcomed to 'poxy Netley'.

The hospital was nearly a mile from the station, and on arrival at the guard room I was helped inside. '23435450 Private Hibbert reporting for duty Sergeant.' 'Relax laddie you're not in training now and you are certainly not fit for duty, the only place you're going is to the medical centre', came the reply. 'You are in D block, the stores will send your bedding, a pair of shoes and company flashes over; I will see you later.'

At the medical centre I was seen by a young doctor (in the RAMC all doctors are officers). The long journey had made my foot swell even larger. 'That looks painful'. 'It is sir'. An x-ray confirmed Dr Pickard's diagnosis that it wasn't broken, but there were badly torn ligaments. I was strapped up, issued with a pair of crutches and a four day 'excused all duties' chit, advised complete rest and told to report back on Monday after the Commanding Officer's interview. All that happened that day was unbelievable; for the first time in months I was treated like a human being and in spite of the pain I began to feel much better.

To service the hospital patients and staff, there was a large Army Catering Corps contingent at Netley and the food was reasonable. Over the weekend I began to make friends and find my way around on my crutches. The old hospital building was over half a mile long, and was, with the exception of the theatre and church, largely unused. The empty main corridors were wide enough to drive ambulances down; the hospital was built under the supervision of Florence Nightingale, then during the First World War was occupied by the British army, and in the Second World War by the Americans. The main building was on the banks of Southampton Water with well kept lawns sloping down to the water's edge where I would sit looking in awe at the large liners sailing past, including the Queen Mary, on their way in and out of Southampton Port. The occupied part of the hospital was a series of widely scattered single storey buildings built in the early 1950s.

Little did I think then that in 39 years time my wife and I would sail down Southampton Water on the liner Oriana on the occasion of our 60th birthdays. Today the original hospital grounds have been transformed into a beautiful country park popular with picnickers who wave at the cruise liners. All that is left of the original Florence Nightingale hospital is the church which is now a museum and visitors' centre, and all traces of the 'newer' hospital have disappeared.

As a result of my injury I could not commence the hospital ward posting, which was duly cancelled, and I was transferred to a 4 week trooping pool training course. My ankle injury was indeed fortuitous, for the Netley based trooping pool was possibly the most sought after posting in the British Army. Initially the course involved a lot of classroom work, during which my ankle injury steadily improved, and when not in class I was seconded to light duties in the officers' mess in the evenings and at weekends when not on leave. This got you out of guard duty and lots of other fatigues.

The course was run by QAs. (Queen Alexandra's Royal Nursing Corps). All QA sisters are officers. The senior QA was a Sister Tutor, equivalent to a hospital matron, who would stand no nonsense and was both respected and feared by her pupils and by the doctors who came to lecture.

During the course we learned about TB and horrible tropical diseases we had never heard of, along with the treatment and nursing of infectious diseases. Great emphasis was placed on the importance of preventing shiploads of sex-starved troops catching sexual diseases, affectionately known as 'knob rot'. At every port of call where shore leave was granted F.F.I. (free from infection) procedures were rigorously enforced in the mistaken belief that this would keep the troops healthy and prevent them from fertilizing the local female population. In reality it did not work, mainly because the regulation issue 'French letters' were like bicycle inner tube tyres and invariably finished up in the harbour straight away. In their lectures the QAs placed great emphasis on the importance of abstinence, but it was very much a case of 'not practising what you preach'. But then they had access to penicillin!

The Sister Tutor was obsessed with bowels, she would impress on all her pupils and the poor patients in the wards that the most important part of all nursing was the inducement and recording of bowel movements. Her motto was 'if bowels are not working efficiently then the body is not working efficiently, a healthy body has healthy bowel movements'. Under no circumstances could a patient be discharged from hospital until they have regular 'movements'. I wrote in my note book: 'If you haven't been you can't go'.

Life at Netley was enjoyable; if you could afford it you could go home most weekends, a monthly travel warrant was issued at the CO's discretion. I was very fortunate that while on my first weekend's leave from Netley and in the Holly Bush Inn in Bollington I met a very nice gentleman by the name of Arthur Jones. Arthur was managing director of Jones Printers in Bollington and Millbrook Press Ltd. in Southampton. Most Fridays Arthur would drive from Southampton to Bollington returning on Sunday afternoons and he offered me a lift whenever I could get a weekend leave pass.

During the trooping pool course and while working in the Officers' Mess I joined the theatre group as a volunteer stage-hand operating the stage lighting. Concerts were regularly given for both the benefit of patients and staff, and residents of Netley village would also be invited. Professional artists would perform free of charge.

It was at a concert featuring a group called the 'Springfields' that I met Dusty Springfield. After the show there was a back stage party, and fuelled by a combination of vodka and scrumpy there was much merriment and dancing. I remember kissing Dusty, but I was extremely drunk and my memories of the details are hazy. What I do know is that next morning I felt seriously ill, and it lasted for two days. Death seemed to be infinitely preferable to what I was suffering; Southampton Water looked extremely inviting. Over the next few days I slowly recovered, and I have never touched a drop of vodka since that concert party or even been drunk again. Now whenever I hear or see the late Dusty Springfield it brings back fond but cloudy memories.

A famous visitor to Netley while I was there was Terry Dean, the 1950s pop idol, but he was not there to entertain - he was a patient. Terry was having problems coping with national service. A large number of photographers and 'teeny boppers' camped outside the gates for days, and we were strictly forbidden to talk to the press under any circumstances. He was eventually discharged from the army.

I successfully completed the trooping pool course and was attached to the M.S. Dunera which was based at Southampton Port. The first voyage was to be to the Far East via the Suez Canal calling at Gibraltar, Malta, Cyprus, Aden, Ceylon, Singapore and Hong Kong.

CHAPTER IV
M.S. DUNERA

There were about seven troop ships operating in the 1950s, five on 'deep sea' routes, and two smaller vessels that did nightly crossings of the North Sea between Harwich and the Hook of Holland (for Germany). Very few military, consular or embassy staff were transported by air. All the troop ships were civilian vessels chartered by the MOD, the crew including the captain were merchant navy with a limited number of military permanent staff. My first ship the M.S. (merchant ship) Dunera, along with her sister ship the M.S. Dilwara, were both of 12,612 tons and owned by the British Indian Steamship Navigation Company. Not being large boats they pitched and rolled alarmingly in bad weather, and lacking the comforts of the larger troop ships such as the Navasa they were not popular with either staff or passengers.

The crew were predominately Indian with white officers, permanent military personnel consisted of a major who was ship's commandant (OIC), two RAPC (Royal Army Pay Corps) clerks, one RAMC captain (doctor), two QA captains (ward sisters and female nursing), one RAMC sergeant (pharmacist), one RAMC warrant officer (administration), four RAMC privates (general duties) and one company sergeant major (discipline). In addition any military passengers such as surgeons, dentists, midwives, redcaps (military police) and even civilian entertainers could be seconded for

Bar life on the Dunera.

Ward life on the Dunera.

duties by the OIC or the doctor. Alcohol was freely available at the ship's bars and NAAFI, except when in territorial waters, and inter-regimental rivalry was fanatical - consequently the redcaps could be very busy. The ship's captain, in accordance with maritime law, was in overall command; this was a unique situation, in that a civilian could give orders to senior military officers.

British Army, Naval, and RAF personnel were transported in addition to diplomatic staff plus the armed forces of other friendly countries visiting the UK for training or medical treatment. Accommodation for officers, civilians, their wives and children was in individual outside cabins, other ranks wives and their children were in inside cabins, subject to rank and availability, with the exception of officer's husbands who slept in the dormitories with conjugal visits permitted at prearranged times. Rank structure was strictly observed with separate messes and bars for officers and NCOs, permanent medical staff were allowed to use the sergeants' mess and the crews bar, but only because we were safer there and wouldn't get involved in the brawls.

The medical facilities consisted of a general ward of about 16 beds situated mid-ships with two adjacent double staff cabins, heads (toilets) and a sluice room, operating theatre, a consulting room that doubled up as a dental surgery and doctor's office, pharmacy, sister's office that doubled as a female examination room and a small female ward. There were two padded cells for the incarceration of violent mental patients - if you weren't mad when you were locked in one of these you soon were - about eight foot square they were the most claustrophobic thing I have ever encountered. A twelve bed isolation ward was situated on the top deck at the stern and there were also prison cells in the bows that we occasionally had to visit. This was 'my home' for the next twelve months.

Like today's cruise liners, the departure from Southampton was a grand and nostalgic occasion with a military band playing stirring music, tears flowing freely as relations and girlfriends waved goodbye. Many of the regular troop and their families could be away for a considerable time; the national service contingents were not allowed to take wives and would spend most of the next two years overseas. (And in 1958 there was no hopping on a flight home).

As we sailed down Southampton Water for the first time I, like many others, stood at the ships rails wondering if we would ever see England again;

my only previous experience of going over seas was crossing the Menai bridge to Anglesey. This was 1958, very few of the hundreds of troops on board would have been abroad, these were the days of holidays at Butlins, the Costa del Sol had yet to be discovered.

We soon settled down to a routine of lifeboat drills and ship's inspections, on outward sailings it was relatively quiet in the hospital. The only patients were the odd appendicitis, sea sickness, fight related injuries, toothache or sunburn. Serious cases of sunburn were a major problem for, in spite of the daily warnings, men would fall asleep on deck for a relative short period - no one had heard of sun cream then - and wake up with extensive blistering and dehydration. The more serious cases had to be transferred to on shore hospitals. Strong sunlight and heat was completely new to most of us, and on entering the Mediterranean reminders were published in daily orders. Open deck was initially restricted to five minutes a day, increasing as we became more acclimatised, and sunburn was a chargeable offence, dealt with as 'self inflicted injuries'. Many patients on the daily sick parade were suffering from prickly heat; the standard treatment was to cover the effected area with calamine lotion, and in severe case a calamine lotion bath was necessary. Most injuries were the result of fighting or rough weather and there was always at least one shooting accident a week through weapon training and sea target practice.

Other routine work included the never ending runs of inoculations and vaccinations. All military personnel on board were to have several of these during the voyage, and every seven days all personnel had an FFI (Free From Infection inspection, which involved close examination for signs of tinea pedis (athletes foot), prickly heat, sexual diseases, and head and pubic nits, lice and mites. Other ranks would line up in four rows in their shorts, dropping them for the more intimate part of the proceedings, if anything suspicious was found you would refer then to the MO. Officers had their FFIs in private by the MO and females were examined by the QAs.

On homeward voyages it was completely different. The hospital would be full with patients returning for further treatment, the isolation ward would be full, often with Gurkhas being transferred to the UK for TB treatment. The relaxed atmosphere of 'coming home' with demob in sight for many after years in foreign lands, meant many more drink-related injuries - and more so if there were Scottish regiments on board. Another problem on return trips

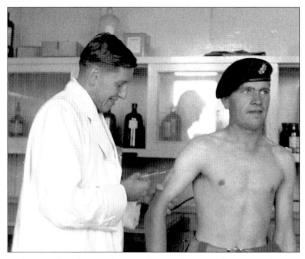

were the number of miscarriages brought on by rough weather; many pregnancies had not been disclosed in case home-coming was delayed.

With more troop ships than cruise ships shore leave could be an important part of a country's economy particularly for a port's female population. Before any shore passes were issued there would be a lecture on how not to catch VD and maps of 'out of bounds' (OOB) areas were displayed on notice boards. This had the opposite effect to that intended with everyone heading straight for the OOBs. These areas were patrolled by redcaps - it only made you wonder what they were up to! Other advice was how not to be conned into buying the local crap souvenirs - which we all did of course.

It was the duty medic's job to issue anti-infection packs consisting of one French letter (condom) made out of recycled inner tubes and just about as thick, a small tube of antiseptic cream that stung like hell and designed to kill any sexual urge stone dead, and a leaflet telling you to abstain. When the thickness of the MOD condom was discovered they were invariably thrown away and basic urges would take over, to be later regretted

The first port of call was always Gibraltar for mail and fresh water, but no shore leave was granted on outward sailings due to the popularity of going AWOL and disappearing across the border into Spain. On home bound journeys it was different and huge quantities of cheap cigarettes would be purchased most of which would be confiscated by the posse of customs officers that would come on board at Gibraltar and sail with the ship to Southampton. We used to do very well - the first personnel to disembark were the stretcher cases and under every blanket would be cigarettes, whisky and cameras. I still have an Agfa camera bought in Aden for £1.10s and smuggled between a stretcher patient's legs.

Malta was the next stop and the first chance for shore leave. With contraception then illegal in Malta, FFI kits were not issued - something that no one told me about until I had given out approximately 200 kits causing a 'diplomatic' incident involving the local police and church officials. Many of the kits were recovered but some were sold down the 'gut' at a full profit. I did not like Malta, it seemed to rain on every visit and there were always American warships in Valetta harbour which would inflate the price of everything including getting ashore when the local water taxis would demand more money when halfway between ship and shore. It was nearly always necessary to threaten to overturn the elegant gondola-like boat or beat up the rower. In Valetta hoards of children were always collecting for the RSPCA or some other well-known 'charity'! Unfortunately unless you happened to be posted to Malta there was never any time to explore the island.

Cyprus was a dangerous place in the 1950s. With the EOKA terrorist war at its height, we anchored off Famagusta where lighters came alongside to disembark the hundreds of troops posted there to keep the peace. It seemed that half the ships company were leaving us at Cyprus. There was a tragic incident on my first visit to Cyprus when a RAF lad complete with full kit fell off the lighter and went to the bottom 'like a stone'. In spite of gallant attempts the water was too deep for any hope of rescue and Naval divers would later recover the body. Due to the terrorist threat there was no shore leave at Cyprus but on homeward sailings we did get ashore, and issued with a revolver with six rounds and with an armed escort we would collect casualties by ambulance from the BMH. The irony was that we were instructed not to use the revolvers.

Drinking water was often a problem particularly on the long drag between Cyprus and Ceylon (Sri Lanka) - no drinkable water was available at Port Said, Suez or Aden, and contaminated water could spread diarrhoea through the ship in hours. When the water barge came alongside at Famagusta, in addition to the ships tanks every hospital bath and utensil was filled, and with the relative calm of the Southern Mediterranean, the Suez Canal and the Red Sea spillage was not a problem. This water was used first.

We would always arrive at Port Said at dawn ,when ships of all shapes and sizes gathered in convoy in preparation for the journey through the Suez Canal, and as the morning mist lifted the ghost like superstructures of ships sunk during the Suez conflict would slowly emerge from the fog, a reminder that war was never far away, in fact British ships had only just began to use the canal again after a huge dredging and clearance operation following the Suez war.

Local traders in their hundreds in small boats milled around the ship selling everything from fruit to black and white dirty photographs - it was strictly forbidden to buy them but many found their way on board. Currency was never a problem for unlike today sterling was an international currency in much demand. Another trading currency was Woodbines which were far superior to the local camel dung cigarettes. Those of us on our first trip had little idea about exchange rates and £1 could be worth 'thousands' of local currency units, but we soon learned the hard way.

Before entering the canal all weapons and cameras had to be concealed but this did not stop me taking some photographs. My memories of the canal are of seeing a Herbert Lomas Bedford ambulance, on which I had worked as an apprentice, outside the Suez Canal Company's offices at Ismalia and it made me feel very home sick. I will always remember, on the banks of the canal, miles from any civilisation, there was a remote shack with camels tethered outside, a small generator running and a sign that read in English 'Ice cold Coca-Cola'. Further along the canal a crowded train emerged from a dust cloud, passing the ship with all the passengers waving enthusiastically.

THE SUEZ CANAL.

Other lasting images for me were the heat and flies, and the eerie experience, where the canal divides, of ships upper structures travelling in the opposite direction moving silently through the sand dunes with no water in sight.

When we left the canal at Suez we were met by a Royal Naval warship to escort us through the Red Sea. The Red Sea is flanked by the deserts of Saudi Arabia, Sudan and Ethiopia and incredibly hot, although the Dunera had air blower louvres it was not air-conditioned. With no shooting practice or other on deck activities possible due to the heat, boredom as well as dehydration were a problem. A feature of the Red Sea are the currents, the sea appears calm but the swell made the ship roll and this caused more sea sickness than the Bay of Biscay. At the narrow southern exit to the Red Sea lies Djibouti on the Ethiopian side and Aden on the Yemeni side. You could smell Steamer Point Aden from miles out at sea. Aden was a British garrison, and at that particular time was relatively safe - safe enough for a short period on shore. The cheapest cameras in the world could be purchased in Aden - and that was about the only good thing that could be said about it.

Steamer Point, Aden

After the Gulf of Aden you keep 'left' for the Arabian Sea, the Persian Gulf and the Gulf of Oman, or fork right into the Indian Ocean. At the foot of India lies Ceylon (Sri Lanka) with its capital Colombo. What a morale booster Colombo was, with its green palm trees, London double deck buses (still with London Transport on the sides), Woolworths, friendly cafes and cold Tiger beer. With fresh water, provisions and less than half of the original contingent on board it was now an enjoyable sail through the Andaman Sea down the Strait of Malacca and coast of Sumatra to Singapore.

At Singapore we were given the opportunity of a two night break at the Changi transit camp built on the site of the notorious Changi Japanese prisoner of war camp, and now one of the most beautiful airports in the world (see chapter IX). Just across the causeway from Changi lay Malaya and the Viet Cong guerillas; many of the troops that had disembarked at Singapore would soon be in armed conflict with them.

From Singapore it was across the South China Sea to Hong Kong and a four-day turnaround break at the BMH. It is now difficult to imagine how Hong Kong looked in the 1950s; about the only things that have not changed are the trams on Hong Kong Island, the Star Ferry and the firing of the Noon Day Gun (see chapter XIV). Little did I dream what an important part in my life Hong Kong would play twenty five years later.

After this spell of long distance trooping I was promoted to the dizzy rank of lance corporal and seconded to the Port of Harwich transit camp. Here with nightly sailings to the Hook of Holland with troops and families posted to Germany, with only two medical staff you were very much on your own during the crossings relying entirely in serious emergencies on in-transit doctors and radio advice. The boats were much smaller than the deep sea troop ships and with the North Sea gales it was much rougher than anything I had previously encountered, and particularly on winter nights, we would always be busy with a wide range of accidents and illnesses.

During all of my two years in the army, apart from when in the Far East, I never encountered drugs.

The last few months of my National Service were spent as the OIC, Corporal of the REME training camp medical centre at Blandford Forum, where I had my own room, telephone and a driver, and it was while on leave from Blandford that I met a girl called Elsie Green at the Regal ballroom Alderley Edge. On 14th December 1959 I said farewell to the army, and Elsie and I married on March 18th 1961.

Our newly married life was fun; most of our leisure time involved the Cavendish Car Club in Macclesfield. We had a series of Minis in which we competed with some success in trials and rallies, but following a heavy encounter with a stone wall on Biddulph Moor and with a baby on the way I was 'persuaded' to give it up, and when Jane was born we went 'up market' and bought an Austin A40.

CHAPTER V
CHESHIRE FIRE BRIGADE

After leaving the army I returned to Herbert Lomas Ltd and following a soul-destroying spell in the car sales division reverted, at my own request, back to the shop floor to practice my electrical trade in the ambulance manufacturing division. I remained at Lomas's for another uneventful 17 years. Outside work things were more exciting; Elsie presented us with a lovely baby daughter, Amanda Jane, in 1965 and a son, Peter Jonathan, in 1970.

I floundered as the works 'first aider' so I went on a St. John's Ambulance course held at Wilmslow Fire Station. Halfway through the first session the station fire bells 'went down' for a fire call and the siren sounded to call in the retained (part-time) firemen. There were five full-time firemen (the duty watch) and several retained firemen on the first aid course, and they all jumped up and ran across the yard to the appliance bay. The first fire engine a P.E. (Pump Escape) drew out of the station and headed for Wilmslow town centre with its bell ringing, the second machine a WRT (Water Tender) followed shortly after manned by the retained crew. This was all very exciting, I immediately decided 'this was for me' and I was going to become a retained fireman.

I duly applied and was sent to my doctor for a very rudimentary medical. Dr Walsh listened to my heart, asked me how I felt and that was it; there was no mention of the hay fever and asthma I had suffered since leaving the army. Two weeks later I reported to Wilmslow fire station on a Wednesday evening drill night to be kitted out and to meet the other retained firemen. After several weeks of quite basic training I was given the go ahead to go 'on the run' and the GPO installed a call bell in my home. Unlike today, breathing apparatus and other specialised training was not undertaken until you had ground experience - fire fighting was learned the hard way at the sharp end.

Fire sirens only sounded from 0700hrs to 2300hrs, call bells in the home worked 24 hours a day, and three days after I went 'on the run' the house bell rang and the siren wailed. It was my first shout (fire call), Corporal Jones would have been proud of me, 'Don't panic! Don't panic Mr Mannering! I turned around several times, could not find the car keys even though they were hung by the door in readiness, the ignition key didn't want to fit, and when I did get the car to start, against all the advice and orders, I drove to the fire station like a maniac. In years to come as a junior officer I would severely reprimand young firemen for this sort of reckless behaviour.

The call was to a grass fire at Cheadle, and with Cheadle's and Wilmslow's first machines out on other jobs this meant a long run to the job. One thing you do not learn in training is the art of getting dressed into your fire gear in the rear cab of a moving fire engine travelling at speed, with four other men all trying to do the same thing. I can only describe it as like a scene from a 'Carry On' film with feet frequently in someone else's Wellingtons. We went through Handforth with the Leading Fireman in the front seat furiously ringing the bell as if his life depended on it. The Dennis F8 Wrt with its Rolls Royce straight 8 cylinder petrol engine averaged less than two miles per gallon. 55mph could be achieved on a good run, and with 400 gallons in the water tank, no power steering, no synchromesh gears, poor brakes and an offset steering wheel, it took lot of skill to drive the beast. Using beaters the grass fire was quickly dealt with and I would be paid ten shillings and sixpence for this exciting experience.

After two years at Wilmslow we moved home to Bollington where I transferred to the local station (B6), which was a wholly retained station with no full time firemen. It was an important part of the community and therefore much more rewarding and exciting. A fire or special service call on your own 'patch' was 'yours' and did not 'belong' to the whole-time firemen. I was to serve at Bollington for a further 23 years becoming a Leading Fireman and acting Sub-officer in charge of the station.

Bollington personnel were responsible for the administration of the station and station area (with the exception of fire prevention legislation) and this included the parishes of Bollington, Prestbury, Kettleshulme, Rainow, Pott Shrigley, Lyme Handley, and Adlington. There were some wonderful sounding locations, Charles Head, Andrews Knob, Pym Chair, Oldgate Nick, Bottom-of-the-Oven, Truggs-in t' Hole, Cats Tor, Hollow cowhey, Penny Loaves and Pott Lords, to name just a few.

When I joined Cheshire Fire Brigade local telephone exchanges put 999 calls through to local manned fire stations, but shortly afterwards central mobilising was introduced transferring the receipt of fire calls from five divisional fire stations to brigade headquarters in Chester. This led to some initial problems with parish locations and the wrong routing of 999 calls   It was not unusual for Bollington to be turned out to an address in Little Bollington near Altrincham, a 999 call to a road accident at Adlington turned out to be Adlington in Lancashire, and a call to a living room fire near Longnor would have meant passing three fire stations, one in Cheshire and two in Derbyshire. On another occasion Cheshire control passed a call to a fire in Wythenshaw Lane, Wincle, to Manchester as a call to Wythenshaw 20 miles away. In similar circumstances a call to a cottage on fire at Bottom-of-the-Oven was passed by Manchester to Cheshire who in turn passed it to Derbyshire who passed it back to Cheshire. Bollington was turned out to Bottom o ' th' Oven in Kettleshulme, the fire turned out to be near New Mills on the Manchester/Derbyshire border. It took us an hour to get there in a blizzard, fortunately the mistake had been realised and a fire engine from Marple had found the cottage which was 'well alight'. As a result of the long drive our snow chains had become loose and it was another two hours before we arrived back at station, very tired, wet and cold. The Dennis F28 was not fitted with a heater and at that time our fire tunics were not waterproof.

How do you summarise 25 years in the fire service with thousands of calls, not to mention the comradeship and social life? I will tell you just a few of the more interesting and amusing incidents. Fatal fires were fortunately not common; in 25 years I only attended 7 or 8 fatal fires, carried out only one personal rescue and was involved in just another three. However I've lost count of the many fatal road accidents I attended.

Fire fighting can be dangerous and while there must have been many occasions I should have been frightened I can only recollect three incidents that were truly frightening. The first was while fighting a large fire at Wellington Mill, Hazel Grove (a twenty pump fire). I, with many others, was manning branches (water jets) from the roof of an adjoining building, and as the walls and roof of the mill and walls began to collapse we realised we had nowhere to run - and you can not just let go of a fire hose charged at 100psi without causing serious injury. We managed to lash the hose and got to the ground just in time to see the walls collapse. Another dangerous incident was at Victory Mill, Park Green, Macclesfield. The top floors of the five story mill were 'well alight', and I was working a monitor from the top of Macclesfield's 100 foot TL (turn table ladder) without a safety belt. I tried to secure myself with my belt line but my hands were so cold that I could not tie the knots - looking down into an inferno from a rocking 100 foot very old Bedford turn table ladder is a very good cure for constipation. The officer that ordered me up the ladder with out a safety belt is now deceased and it would not happen in today's fire service. While the two top floors of the mill were gutted the rest of the mill was saved, and this incident was a good example of aggressive fire fighting with a good 'stop'. The remaining three floors are still in use today.

Another incident I remember well involved an overturned car outside the Cock and Pheasant pub in Bollington. I crawled inside the car to comfort the woman who was trapped while the rest of the crew organised the rescue. The car was swimming in petrol and in spite of a covering jet I remember thinking 'if this fires up we are both 'barbecued'!'

In 25 years I only required the services of Macclesfield's hospital casualty department on three occasions. A cut hand required stitching, a foreign body in the eye and in the early hours of one Sunday morning multiple wasp stings - but that is another story.

Many amusing incidents would start before reaching the fire station. With many of the firemen working shifts, being aroused by the call bell or alerter from a deep sleep, getting dressed on the way to the fire station still half asleep can have curious effects. Many responded on bicycles and the site of a fireman peddling furiously through the village in broad daylight with his trousers on back to front showing the cheeks of his bum to the village was not unknown. One fireman's son was notorious for the time he loosened the nuts on the front wheel of his dad's bike - poor Harold dashed out of the house grabbed his bike and went over the handle bars in the street. And responding by car in the middle of the night on icy roads was hazardous and more than one Bollington fireman would find himself in the hedge in Albert Road.

But Bollington's firemen were very professional, dedicated, compassionate and extremely experienced, and in addition to their own station area calls they attended all the major incidents in Macclesfield and throughout the county.

Alerter electronic call out units eventually replaced the house call bells and siren, and shortly after their introduction I was outside the fire station which was near to my home early one evening when my bleeper sounded. At that very moment my wife ran down our house drive waving her arms and shouting. I shouted back, 'Don't serve my tea out, we've got a shout' and with that I ran to the station watch room to get the call address from the teleprinter. (Mobilising was from brigade HQ at Chester). The address read 'Kitchen fire 68 Albert Road, Bollington', 'This has to be a false alarm' I said, nevertheless I wasn't waiting and with just a crew of two I drove the fire engine the few yards to my home - the rest of the lads could respond on foot. Thick black smoke was bellowing out of the back door, Elsie had left the chip pan on while attending to our baby son, and the kitchen and fittings were 'gutted' with smoke damage throughout the house. A few days later the local newspaper carried the following report:

PERSONAL FIRE CALL
Mr Graham Hibbert, a Bollington fireman turned out with the rest of the Brigade on Thursday when there was a call to his own home, 68 Albert Road, only yards from the Fire Station. He hoped it was a false alarm but the crew found the kitchen a mass of flames. The blaze which started when a chip pan was left on the electric cooker, caused extensive damage.

(Ironically many years later, long after I had retired from the fire service, I would be designing chip pan fire demonstration units)

Probably the largest fire in the North West of England since the Manchester blitz, was Texas Mill, Ashton-Under-Lyme, one of the largest mills in the country. Ashton at that time was in Lancashire with nearby Hyde and Stalybridge in Cheshire, and the bordering brigades of Stockport, Manchester, and West Yorkshire were all independent separate fire brigades. There would be seven different fire brigades attending this fire.

Bollington was mobilised late on Saturday evening as part of a 50 Pump 'make up', several hours after the initial call when multiple rescues had been carried out by Lancashire crews. The initial crews from Lancashire, Cheshire and Manchester were now exhausted. In normal circumstances this call would have been of great excitement but the mood was sombre, we already knew from the radio messages that a Manchester fireman was lying dead in the inferno.

Five miles from Ashton we could see the fire which at this stage still had 100 foot flames. On arrival we reported to the main control unit and were allocated tasks in one of the four sectors. Over 300 firemen were using

FIREMAN DIES IN MILL BLAZE TEXAS GUTTED

MORE THAN 200 EMPLOYEES of the Texas Mill, Ashton, will probably lose their jobs following the disastrous fire which began on Friday and raged over the weekend. One fireman lost his life and five others were injured.

Fireman Norman Nolan, aged 28, a member of the Manchester City Fire Brigade was killed in the gutted six-storey building. Sub-Officer William Partington, of Mossley, was badly hurt.

30 jets, and we were working in several inches of warm run off water. Appliances from as far away as Preston and Lancaster were arriving. But around the Salvation Army mobile canteens there was no witty camaraderie or frivolity; it was several days before Fireman's Nolan's body was recovered. Not all the pumps' crews would be involved in direct fire fighting; many would be engaged in essential water relays necessary to pump around 5000 gallons (22,500 litres) of water a minute to the fire ground.

Unlike 'make up' pumps which are always mobilised from the nearest stations irrespective of county boundaries, a Brigade will always try to supply relief pumps from its own resources, and next morning the Bollington crew were relieved by a pump from Morecambe. The logistics of such a huge fire in providing pumps, relief crews, and fire cover were enormous, but they were always carried out with great efficiency - and without the aid of computers.

With many large mills in North Cheshire 20 pump fires were not unusual, and to attend such large fires was always an exciting experience. Bollington's crews attended many, including the oil refineries at Ellesmere Port. Turnouts to relief duties at major incidents were common.

Bollington would be called out about 700 times a year with most calls outside the station area. The most common incident was grass fires and while some could last for days the majority were quickly 'knocked' - and each one meant a separate call out fee. In August 1976, following the summer drought, Bollington were turned out 118 times, mostly to grass fires. Cheshire along with many other counties was so desperate for machines, at times every fire engine in the county could be committed and on occasions you could be sent to a fire in the Land Rover (L4P) with only two men and little chance of back up.

A tragic fire was at the Mere Golf and Country Club at Knutsford. It was snowing heavily when we were turned out in response to the 'make up'. The large stately building had been well alight when the first crews from Knutsford had arrived, and the wife of the club manager had been reported missing, last seen at a window shouting for help. Damping down the collapsed building you secretly hoped it would not be you that came across the body. She was found later the following day.

I mentioned earlier a personal rescue, something that very rarely happens. Rescues like fire fighting are usually a result of teamwork. With a crew of four we turned out to Greenfield Road, Bollington; on arrival smoke was pouring from the house and the 70 year old occupant (who we all knew) was missing. The OIC and two fireman went to the rear to break in and effect a rescue via the back door, so as driver/pump operator I was at that stage on my own at the front of the house when the bedroom window opened and a youth appeared shouting for help. An excitable crowd had gathered and were all pointing to him. As I grabbed the short extension ladder and pitched it to the window I could hear the two tones of Macclesfield's pump coming through the village but still several minutes away - this was my moment of glory; I must rescue him before they arrive. I was half way up the ladder wondering if I could carry him down when he got on to the ladder himself and started coming down on his own like a 'scalded cat'. I remember thinking 'go back I'm supposed to rescue you'! The onlookers clapped as the youth got to the ground, but he was an intruder and quickly disappeared into the crowd and was never identified. I felt robbed, but thankfully - and most importantly - the occupier was successfully rescued and made it to the Royal Oak that night!

Another rescue worthy of note was that of 14 schoolgirls trapped in a minibus in deep snow drifts at Pott Shrigley during a blizzard. All 14 girls, the driver and two firemen all ended up squeezed into the Redwing Land Rover that had a seating capacity of five. It was not unusual for the Land Rover to be turned out to rescue motorists trapped in the snow and to assist the police. The Redwing, registration number 588AMB, has long since gone to a well-earned retirement - but is still in excellent condition and is preserved by the owner in Worcestershire.

In addition to the weekly drill night there were many special training courses including residential courses at the Northern Fire College at Washington Hall in Lancashire and the world famous National Fire Training College at Moreton-in-Marsh. Here you would train alongside firemen from all over the world, and Moreton-in-Marsh village hall had the dubious reputation of holding the best 'grab a granny' nights in the country.

Special Service Calls were nearly always more interesting than fire calls and often required tact and compassion; they included road accidents, workers trapped in machinery including a stone crusher, farmers trapped under tractors and in agricultural machinery, an elderly man with his testicles trapped in the bed springs (ouch), cattle, horses and bulls trapped in cess pits, sheep trapped in quarries and reservoir dam tunnels, a girl with her finger stuck in the wing mirror hole of her car, babies locked in bathrooms, children with fingers stuck in plug holes, people trapped in lifts, people trapped on roofs, little boys stuck up trees, men trapped under their cars, kittens up chimneys, dogs down badger sets, boats sinking in the canal, removal of rings from swollen fingers, naked grooms chained to lamp posts, a couple trapped in their convertible having 'rumpy pumpy' when a cow jumped over a hedge and landed on top of it... and many more including flooding. Flooded houses could be heart-breaking particularly when the elderly were involved, and unless there was danger to life or of fire, flooding

Penny Lane, Rainow.

was a chargeable service.   But I am proud of the fact that never once when I was in charge of a domestic flooding incident was the paperwork processed that would have resulted in charges.

Dawn one lovely summer morning saw a call to the Lamaloud Reservoir Dam at Rainow where a cow was trapped in the fork of an electricity pole support.   There was a blanket of mist in the Lamaloud Valley when we arrived at 5.30am, the incident on high ground some distance from the access lane.   Blackhawk hydraulic rams were got to work, which required timber packing - fencing posts were ideal, and it was while tugging at these in a hedgerow that I disturbed a wasps' nest.   Within seconds I was covered in 'thousands' of them, all hell-bent on personal vengeance for having their Sunday morning 'lie in' disturbed.

There were wasps in my hair, inside my tunic, clinging to my hands and face, in my ears, each one seeking personal revenge for the wrecking of their home.   I ran off, followed by the angry swarm, towards the rest of the crew who were gathered around the unfortunate cow.   But I was definitely not welcome and was very firmly told to 'go away' - or at least that is what was meant - and to take my newly found friends with me.

With that I ran down the field to the pump with the intention of putting my head against the exhaust pipe and using the tank water to wash the b----s off, discarding my tunic as I ran. I emerged from the mist stripped to the waist and waving my arms about, and shouting obscenities. At this point a lone hiker emerged from the mist walking up the lane without a care in the world. He took one look at me, turned around and headed back towards Rainow as fast as his legs would carry him, convinced he was being attacked by a maniac.

Just as I had finished my road side ablutions the RSPCA man arrived in response to our team's request about the cow. 'You look a mess - we had better sought you out first,' he said. I stared in horror at the humane killer in his hand and was relieved when he said 'The cow can wait, jump in the van and I'll run you to hospital'. 'It's not my day,' I thought, 'anyone else would get an ambulance, I get an RSPCA van with a guy armed with a humane killer'.

On arrival at casualty, rather than ring the emergency door bell we used the side staff entrance. All was quiet in casualty. 'Anyone about' shouted the RSPCA man. A dishevelled Sister emerged from a cubicle followed by a male nurse, not amused at having being disturbed, and told me I should not be out fishing at that time of a morning.

After an injection and a liberal coating of green Anthisan cream I was advised to rest for a few days. With hundreds of stings it was a very painful experience but at least it proved I did not have an allergy to insect stings something that would be useful in my later adventures in Africa.

Occasionally even before arriving at the fire you could sense a real fire (a 'goer'). This was the case one early hours, when as soon as I opened the front door, the bangs from the Bollington Cross Social Club that was 'well alight' were clearly heard. And you did not need an address for fires at Kay's foam factory, you could smell it - 'it's Kay's and it's a 'goer'' we would shout. One night as I glanced out of the bedroom as my bleeper was going I could see a huge glow over the hillside in the direction of Pott Shrigley. Explosions could be clearly heard.

The teleprinter message read 'Wrt & L4P to grass fire in the hills opposite Kay Metzeller Ltd. Bollington'. We looked. This surely couldn't be right? This had to be a crashed aircraft? And the location was incorrect. (A man decorating his lounge in the early hours had seen a glow in the hills). This was to be the largest fire that I would ever be in charge of - until the army of white helmets arrived. It was also one of the most dangerous and most unusual, the story is told in the appendix of radio messages from the fire ground relayed back from control to Bollington's station teleprinter.*

As the years went by there were huge improvements in fire appliance design, protective clothing and rescue equipment. I had a reputation as a good pump operator, and considered myself a good driver - in twenty-five years service I only crashed the fire engine three times, which might sound a lot but when you consider the weather conditions we had to contend with and the poor brakes on the earlier fire engines it was not a bad record. And fortunately, other than pride, there were no injuries.

After twenty years I was awarded the Queen's Long Service and Good Conduct Medal, a royal warrant medal of which I am proud. The last major fire I attended before retiring with arthritis in 1987 was yet another ten pump fire at Kay Metzeller Ltd, this time in the afternoon. In addition to their new warehouse being destroyed thirty employees' cars were burnt out. I could fill many more pages with fire service stories but will finish with a poignant story so unusual that I doubt if it had ever happened before or will ever happen again anywhere in the world.

The funeral of Sub Officer Sid Hartley was held at St. Gregory's Roman Catholic Church in Bollington and station personnel in their best uniforms acted as pall bearers. There were many senior fire officers present. During the last hymn the organ sounded out of tune, and had in fact caught fire but being situated right at the back of the church most of the congregation was blissfully unaware. Station Officer David Makepeace quietly slipped out of church and relayed a fire call to BHQ from his car radio. As the responding appliances approached the church they were ordered to turn off their flashing lights and sirens. The fire was quickly dealt with using portable CO_2 extinguishers.

Then as Sid's coffin was carried from church, the attending fire crews stood to attention by their appliance with helmets under their arms. Most of the mourners thought this was part of Sid's ceremonial 'goodbye' Unfortunately the tabloid press got hold of the story and next morning's Daily Mirror read 'FIRE CHIEF GOES OUT IN BLAZE OF GLORY', Needless to say Sid's widow, affectionately known as Aunty Mary, was not amused.

In the months and years to come my fire service training and experience would 'open many doors' worldwide.

* NAB QUARRY FIRE SUNDAY JUNE 21ST 1981

0234   Two appliances Bollington ordered to fire in the hills above Bollington.
0245   Radio message 'Priority, from Leading fireman Hibbert at corrected address
        Nab Quarry Pott Shrigley, make pumps four'
        Two pumps Poynton ordered.
0251   Radio message 'Priority, from Leading Fireman Hibbert make pumps six.'
        Two pumps Macclesfield, emergency tender Crewe, control unit ordered.
0256   Radio message 'From Leading Fireman Hibbert, informative message. Two
        separate incidents involving brick processing plant, storage sheds, several
        lorries and drums of unknown chemicals, both incidents well alight. Person
        throwing rocks at fire fighters from top of quarry face. Two main jets in use.
0308   Radio message 'From ADO Halley, make pumps eight, hydraulic platforms one'
        One pump Wilmslow, one pump Whalley Bridge & HP Macclesfield ordered.
0348   Radio message, 'From DO Blenkinsop. Make pumps ten'
        One pump Congleton, one pump GMC, petrol carrier Crewe ordered.
        Divisional Commander going on.

The fire was eventually brought under control by four main jets, hydraulic platform
monitor, several hose reels, all fed from a twin two mile up hill relay from the canal.
Breathing apparatus and chemical protection suites were used throughout. Relief crews
were brought in from all over the county and were in attendance for two days. Police
toured surrounding farms warning of the danger from toxic smoke and there was a
constant update on wind speed and direction from Manchester Airport weather centre.

    The cause of the fire was arson with three seats of fire using accelerants; in spite
of an extensive CID investigation no arrests were made. The man throwing stone was
believed to be a well known local eccentric who live rough near by, he was not charged.

Working from the turntable ladder at Gradus Mill, Macclesfield.

Road traffic accidents were common.

Plastic granules on fire at Grimshaw Lane, Bollington.

Thirty cars ablaze alongside warehouse at Bollington.

Climbing the turntable ladder at Gradus Mill.

Ten pump fire at Berrisford's Mill, Macclesfield.

Inspecting London Fire Brigade's new Metz turntable ladder.

CHAPTER VI
CHESHIRE FIRE ENGINEERING LTD

I was 39, working on a factory shop floor as an auto electrician in the ambulance manufacturing industry. I had two children, and yes I had the excitement of the fire brigade call-outs but still I felt I was getting 'nowhere', I had never flown and with the exception of a short excursion to Brittany had never had an overseas holiday. All that was about to change.

No one ever left Lomas's of their own accord, you were either sacked, retired (well after retirement age) or died. It was after attending a succession of workers funerals that I started to get very restless and decided that after 23 years in the same job, it was time to move on. But where?

Browsing though 'Fire International' magazine one day, I spotted an advert for a quality control engineer at ERF Fire Engineering Ltd, later to become Cheshire Fire Engineering Ltd (CFE). A subsidiary of the ERF lorry building company the Winsford based fire engine manufacturer built first line fire engines, rescue tenders, turn table ladders, hydraulic platforms and other special fire appliances for the United Kingdom and export.

As an auto-electrician I had no engineering experience, I had virtually no idea what a quality control engineer was and I did not even have a CV, nor did I have any education certificates. I stood no chance of getting an interview let alone the job, so why on earth I applied I will never know. The only possible thing in my favour was my practical fire fighting experience, I was a good driver with a heavy goods licence and an experienced fire pump operator. It turned out that people who designed and built fire engines were not experienced with their ultimate use, ie fire fighting. It was still a big surprise two weeks later to receive a letter inviting me to Winsford for an interview.

It was a very hot and humid day when, in my funeral suit, I arrived at the ERF factory at Winsford and rang the bell in reception. There was no one about, and I thought 'What on earth am I doing here'. As I turned to leave a voice said 'Can I help you?'

The interview was a very nervous affair, but it fortunately concentrated more on the practical use of fire engines, vehicle building and electrics, all subjects of which I had experience and knowledge. After a while I began to relax, a tour of the factory followed with visits to the modern drawing office and the huge stores. Should I get the job it was explained that I would be the departmental head with a staff consisting of a foreman, a driver/fitter and an inspector. My department would be responsible for the quality control, testing and commissioning of all the fire appliances manufactured, some like hydraulic platforms costing in access of £100,000. No fire engine could be delivered or handed over to a customer without clearance by the head of QA. A daunting responsibility. All 'goods inward' were also the Quality Control department's responsibility, and as department head I would be answerable only to the managing director.

It was also explained that I would be expected to attend the company's training school at Sandbach to learn company procedures (they were obsessed with them). I would also have to go on a training course to Simon Engineering at Dudley to learn how to operate and test hydraulic platforms, I would attend other specialised courses and I would be expected to travel overseas commissioning fire engines.

The salary would be more than three times what I was earning at Herbert Lomas, but with applicants from as far a field as London, some with university and engineering degrees, I realised that I did not stand an earthly chance of getting the job anyway.

Two weeks later I received a letter offering me the position, subject to a medical and my willingness to transfer to a 'white collar' union (ERF was very union orientated). I was later to learn that of the other six highly qualified applicants, none had the heavy goods vehicle licence necessary for fire engine driving, some were less enthusiastic at the thought of carrying out testing procedures on ladders and platforms at heights in excess of one hundred feet, and none had fire fighting experience. Courtesy of Cheshire Fire Brigade I had an HGV licence, was not afraid of heights and had fire engine 'hands on' experience. I had also worked in the vehicle building industry for 23 years.

It might be useful to mention here that many people can climb a supported ladder - like a ladder leaning against a wall. But climbing or working from a ladder or aerial platform that is only supported from its base is completely different, it takes considerable nerve and an enormous amount of confidence in the equipment. It can certainly be 'bowel moving' particularly when there is wind sway or technical problems.

It was with both excitement and trepidation that I reported for my first day. How different it was to be. I was issued with a white coat which bore my name and department, I was shown my office, introduced to my staff, the girl who was to be my shared secretary and other senior members of staff. And as I walked through the very long assembly line for the first time all eyes were on the 'new QA manager'. I was introduced to the pension's manager, told how to claim expenses and the procedure for using the car pool. I had not even realised that I would get a pension and other 'perks'.

The first few weeks were relatively easy. I got to know the road testing, pump testing, inspection and other procedures, and the biggest drawback was the amount of paper work, as with many large companies there was far too much paper work with forms and procedures for everything.

Many fireman don't realise that the water they are using to put out a fire has already been used to cool their fire engine. When a fire engine is pumping water, particularly at high pressure on to a fire, some of that water has already passed through intercoolers in the engine, gearbox, power take off and radiator. Electronic and temperature monitoring in all these components was an important part of the testing procedures particularly on appliances for export to hot climate destinations.

The hydraulic platform (HP) course at Simon Engineering was enjoyable with lots of camaraderie with other students, most of whom were fire brigade personnel. With all the students helping each other we all passed the technical tests and I was duly presented with a framed certificate as a qualified Simon 263 HP (26 metre, 3 booms, Hydraulic Platform) operator. Other courses followed including one at Girling concerning a relatively new invention, ABS (antilock braking system) - fire engines were some of the first vehicles to be fitted with ABS.

I became very skilled at demonstrating ABS particularly in the snow, and can honestly say I put 'the fear of god' in many fire brigade engineers on a narrow steep hill near Winsford. ABS was brilliant - until one day when it failed I put a £60,000 fire engine on its side in a ditch. Needless to say I had lots of paperwork to complete. The production supervisor was a lovely man called Jack Borrows, who considering the enormous pressure he was permanently under was always very supportive. I owe him a lot, but he would go 'ape shit' if any defects were found that would interfere with delivery or production schedules and when I crashed the North Yorkshire appliance demonstrating the ABS I thought he was going to have an heart attack. But the chassis and cab were relatively undamaged, Jack and a team of fitters worked through the night to remove the body from another completed fire engine and mount it on the North Yorkshire chassis. The sign writer had just finished the new lettering as the North Yorkshire Fire Brigade engineer arrived to take delivery.

Not long after the Simon course I was sent on my first HP (hydraulic platform) commissioning to Cork in Southern Ireland and this was to prove quite eventful. Much to my astonishment I was told I could take my wife with me, on full company expenses! Four days before Christmas we drove the HP to Fleetwood and embarked on the midnight container vessel to Dublin. Next morning we were met at Dublin Port by the company's Irish agent and taken to a four star hotel to rest in preparation for the drive to Cork the following day. The drive to Cork attracted a lot of attention in the small towns and villages en-route, hydraulic platform fire engines were not a common sight in rural Ireland and whenever we stopped for a break a large crowd would gather.

The firemaster of Cork City Fire Brigade (I will not name him) was a well-known and charismatic character whose grandparents had suffered appallingly at the hands of the British 'Black & Tan' soldiers, and it was noticeable that during the customary 'wining and dining' in a first class hotel that evening he gave generously during the customary collection for the IRA. In fact everyone gave - it would have attracted a lot of unwelcome attention not to.

With the exception of the fire chief damaging the cage on a railway bridge the commissioning went well and two days later we made our way back to Dublin to catch a flight to Manchester. Unfortunately all the flights were over booked and we finished up on the overnight ferry due to arrive in Liverpool on Christmas Eve. The ferry was crowded with Liverpudlians of Irish descent all determined to start Christmas early. It was a rough crossing and it was not long before hoards of drunken moaning bodies started parting company with their stomach contents. Conditions on board were appalling and I vowed never again to cross the Irish Sea by boat.

My next overseas trip was to Amsterdam with White Watch from Paddington Fire Station with an official goodwill visit by London Fire

Testing Nairobi's new hydraulic platform at 100 feet.

Brigade to the Dutch Fire Brigade. ERF at that time built fire engines for the L.F.B. (London Fire Brigade) and had a revolutionary new demonstration fire engine fitted with an American Wateriouse high-pressure pump.

This was to be loaned by ERF to the LFB complete with driver/pump operator (yours truly) for the visit. There were to be drills and fire fighting demonstrations for both the public and civic dignitaries, many civic dinners and receptions, and of course the obligatory 'night out' in the Red Light district including the world famous Kanal Strata.

I was still in Cheshire Fire Brigade at this time but the chief fire officer refused my request to take my fire kit and best uniform on the visit. A real disappointment, but I took them anyway and would have to answer some awkward questions when photographs appeared some time later in national fire magazines.

I drove the fire engine to London to stay overnight at Paddington fire station before the drive next morning to Harwich for the Hook of Holland ferry. At Paddington, Red Watch was on duty. Red Watch and their station officer Neil Wallington had become internationally famous following the recent publication of Gordon Honeycomb's best selling book *Red Watch*, a true account of four days in the life of station A21 (Paddington) culminating with the huge fire at the Worsley Hotel in which seven people were killed. When Red Watch arrived at the hotel many people were trapped with dozens hanging out of windows shouting for help. Some had jumped from their bedroom windows into adjacent trees to escape the flames and were hanging from branches. Multiple rescues were effected from the upper floors of the hotel with the aid of wheeled escape ladders and hook ladders (I used both of these ladders in my early fire service days but they are no longer in fire service use). During the rescue attempts some firemen became trapped and suffered terrible burns; one of them a Red Watch probationary fireman died before he could be rescued.

A warm welcome awaited me at Paddington by both Red Watch and the off duty White Watch. A special meal was laid on in the mess and the station bar provided an endless supply of free beer (there are no longer bars at London fire stations). The highlight of the evening was when I was presented by Gordon Honeycomb with an autographed copy of *Red Watch*. It was the first time any of the firemen at Paddington had had any contact with a real life retained fireman, and their perception of a 'country yokel' with a straw in his mouth attending two or three chimney fires a year was shattered when they learned how many shouts we responded to, the 20 pump mill fires I had attended and the variety of incidents including road accidents I had attended. After the initial cool reception, I was treated with a great deal of respect. That night I was given a bed in the Station Officer's office but had little sleep, - the bells seemed to 'go down' (fire call) and the lights go on at least once an hour.

Next morning with five in the ERF and fifteen in a minibus we set off for Harwich. Unlike the return journey when customs would strip the fire engine and the minibus looking for pornographic films and books (the sort of thing you can now buy at your local newsagent) there were no problems. That is other than finding Y Tunnel 4 fire station in Amsterdam which proved impossible, and we eventually contacted them by phone and were sent a police escort to guide us.

As I would find again many years later the Dutch, unlike the French, were a charming, friendly race. Everyone spoke excellent English and a warm welcome awaited us. That evening, at the first of several receptions, we were each presented with the first of many gifts, a plaster cast fireman in the form of a phallic symbol. The range and amount of fire fighting vehicles at Y Tunnel 4 station was far superior to that found in the UK, and next morning we were taken around the harbour on a fire-fighting tug before the start of the displays in the afternoon.

The evening visit to the red light district was an 'eye opener' - quite unlike the tacky, sleazy and potentially dangerous 'things' I had witnessed in 'the out of bounds areas' in the Far East while in the army. In Amsterdam it was all open with lots of light and lots of tourists. The girls (no boys then) sat naked on display in their windows, you could see the room and bed beyond the curtains - apparently it was important that prospective clients could see into the 'room' to ensure it was clean and had a shower. We found it amusing that when a 'client' came out on to the street the gathered tourists, most of whom were Japanese, would clap, much to his embarrassment. Later that evening we went to a live sex show and were lucky not be arrested when one of the White Watch firemen started a riot by loudly shouting his disapproval at a very crucial moment when a well-endowed coloured man and a white girl were in middle of their act. The audience erupted in protest, the performers fled the stage, the police were called and we all left in a hurry.

I should perhaps add at this point that most of White Watch and myself did not 'sample' anything on offer and with the exception of a few of the younger men, we all returned to our hotel after the show.

The visit was a success, made even more enjoyable for myself by the fact that I was paid for it all, including overtime! When I arrived back at home in the early hours of the next morning I parked up the fire engine in my house drive and the weight fractured the gas main - as well as the ladder breaking our gutter. Needless to say we did not tell the gas company there had been a seven ton fire engine parked on our drive . In spite of my wife's frequent reminders some twenty five years later I still have not got round to replacing the damaged gutter, like most wives she does not seem to appreciate that these thing take time!

After my special leave from Cheshire Fire Brigade it was back to a fire fighting and work routine, but in a few months I would set out for Zanzibar, and this would be the start of a 'love-hate' relationship with Africa. You can often hate it when you are there, but in spite of the many discomforts and problems I came to love the people and developed a strong desire to be helpful to them.

On board a fire-fighting tug in Amsterdam.

CHAPTER VII
ZANZIBAR

Poliomyelitis, hepatitis, tetanus, smallpox, yellow fever, cholera, typhoid, paratyphoid, tuberculosis, diphtheria and meningococcal meningitis were just some of the diseases you had to be vaccinated against before going to Africa. You had to take anti-malaria tablets and there were many other dangers it was wise to be aware of including sexually transmitted diseases (before AIDS) and snake bites. By the time my doctor and the Manchester travel clinic had finished with me I felt as if I had been 'punched bored and countersunk'. Fortunately I had already experienced many of the injections and vaccinations in the army, which undoubtedly helped my body to cope.

Before leaving for Zanzibar there was a commissioning in Inverness returning by air, which would be my first flight experience. I drove the Highland and Islands Fire Brigade Dodge water tender to Inverness in dreadful weather with blizzard conditions, and it was only by following a friendly snow plough driver all the way from Pitlochry to Inverness that I arrived late at night at the Kingsmill Hotel to enjoy a prime Scottish steak and a large 'wee dram'. Fortunately I had thought to drain all the water from the 400-gallon tank and pump, averting any frost damage and I was able to complete the commissioning next day in sub-zero temperatures. That evening the Firemaster Donnie McGlennon and his wife invited me to a caley where for the first time I experienced Scottish country dancing. Scottish dancers must be super fit, not even in the army could I remember such strenuous activity - it was not long before I was completely exhausted.

The next morning I was driven to the then grass strip airport outside Inverness to catch the Logan Air Tri-Lander flight to Glasgow. Before departing Donnie gave me a bottle of pochin, (100% proof illegal whisky) which was the most exhilarating drink I have ever tasted. To this day I can remember even a sip going 'straight down to your toes'.

I was scared stiff even before take off and when we started to be thrown about by the rough weather my heart was literally in my mouth. The small plane was full with 13 passengers, all oil rig workers, all farting freely in the confined space. In hindsight there was little worry as these planes fly in the most appalling weather, and we arrived safely at Glasgow after a hairy landing in gale force winds.

The flight from Glasgow to Manchester on a BAC 111 was completely different and I remember thinking when the free drinks trolley came round 'I could really get to enjoy this'. This visit was the start of my life long love affair with flying and Scotch whisky, my favourite blend is J & B and my favourite single malt is Bowmore; I would come to find and enjoy them all over the world.

A million pound plus credit order supported by the DTI won by CFE to supply the Island of Zanzibar and Pemba with nine fully-equipped Bedford fire engines, five water tenders (Wrt's), two water carriers (WC), two emergency tenders (ET), three Land Rover light fire engines (L4T) and three V.W. ambulances was acclaimed by the press and covered by BBC TV. In reality as I was to realise later this debt-crippling project was a financial disaster for Zanzibar.

At the factory there was lots of euphoria about the contract particularly when the BBC 'Look North' camera and production team arrived. Felicity Goody was the reporter and I was asked as part of the demonstrations to give her a ride in a hydraulic platform while the cameras filmed. She climbed into the cage and quietly asked me not to take her above about head height, every one watching though it was due to the fear of heights but she whispered in to my ear that she was pregnant and that not even her producer was aware of it at that stage, I faked a problem and Felicity only got about 20 foot from the ground instead of the intended 100ft.

Right at the end of the BBC visit Felicity said 'Right Graham we are ready to interview you.' It came out of the blue and I had thirty seconds to straighten my tie before a microphone that looked like a dead rabbit was held just below my waist and I was instructed to look at the camera. 'I understand that you will be going to Zanzibar to teach their firemen how to use these new fire engines and that you are yourself a fireman?' I remember thinking 'this is not fair, I have had no time to think about my answers, and shouldn't we be rehearsing this first'? 'Yes I am looking forward to going to Zanzibar and I am a retained fireman with Cheshire Fire Brigade'. 'Will this help you to do your job?' 'Yes I'm sure it will be a great asset, a great asset.' The rest of the interview is a blur but I do know it was appalling. It went out on Look North that night, and fortunately very few people had video recorders then and I doubt if a copy of the programme exists.

Yes, Zanzibar did desperately need fire engines but not the quantity and type involved. In fairness to Jerry Marsh, the salesman who had obtained the million pounds order and negotiated the DTI, EGCD (Export Guarantee Credit Department) insurance, he did not appreciate the practical difficulties. Getting any order out of Africa was a long complicated process, very often involving practices that had to be handled with great delicacy. The press and the general public would judge these 'practices' to be unethical but they were normal business practice for exporting companies worldwide. I knew little export business procedure at this stage, but in later years I would become quite experienced in dealing with the third world. It was about this time that Brian Smith a director of Dennis, the fire engine chassis manufacturers, was imprisoned in Iran for alleged business 'irregularities'.

Zanzibar, perhaps better known as the spice islands, is a truly beautiful place with warm friendly inhabitants. The national language is Swahili although English is widely spoken, and there is a constant aroma of spice, particularly cloves, in the air. Zanzibar today with the development of tourism is far different than the Zanzibar of 1980. Then there was only one reasonable hotel, and even there, there was a desperate shortage of basic commodities such as soap, toothpaste and even toilet paper, the electricity supply frequently failed and a military style force, known, as the 'committee for the fulfilment of the revolution' was still active. (More later).

An ex British colony, Zanzibar was ruled by a Sultan until 1963 when he was overthrown in a bloody revolution led by Abied Karume during which many died and Abied Karume became president. The Sultan was given twenty minutes to mercilessly kill his children, wives and himself. Helped by loyal followers, along with his family he escaped by dhow from a secluded beach and eventually reached England to live in exile in Southend. The new self acclaimed President Karume caused outrage in the United Nations when he took a 15 year old white girl as his bride, he was shot dead in 1972 while playing cards in the Bwawani Hotel. (See Frederick Forsyth)

The flight to Zanzibar was my first long haul flight and an exciting adventure, via Frankfurt and Khartoum to Dar-es-Salaam in business class with Lufthansa, flying over the breathtaking snow-capped Mount Kilimanjaro close to the equator on the Kenyan/Tanzanian border. At Dar-es-Salaam I was met by Jerry Marsh who had flown in from the Seychelles, and after an overnight stay at the Kilimanjaro hotel we chartered a private Cessna to fly us the forty miles across the Indian Ocean to the island of Zanzibar. I was excited and terrible naive - I was happily taking photographs at airports without realising that you just do not take photographs at foreign airports. I could have very easily finished up in a stinking prison cell, this was my first visit to Africa and I had an awful lot to learn.

On arrival in Stonetown, the capital of Zanzibar, I found there were no 'firemen', just a bunch of undisciplined and untrained youths in ragged jeans. They had no uniforms or equipment other than one helmet between them, which they took turns to wear, invariably back to front, but in spite of their lack of basic facilities they were eager and friendly. And I never encountered dishonesty amongst these boys.

There were no fire engines or ambulances in working order, no drivers other than one policeman a lovely character called Ami Mohammed, and affectionately known as Mickey Daddy. The only fire station on the island could best be described as an open shed; there was no

command structure or mobilising procedures. At the airport when landing, all looked well with the emergency vehicles lined up on the apron, but closer examination revealed that the crash tender had no gearbox or pump, the foam in the tank had long since solidified. The machine was actually pushed on to the apron daily just for show. Perhaps even worse, the airport's 'emergency ambulance' stood on bricks - it had no wheels. 'Welcome to Africa, Graham!'

I had experienced some problems at Dar-es-Salaam airport but the immigration and health control at the tiny Zanzibar airport was amusing to say the least. The man responsible for health and immigration was a very nice guy called Ali who I later got to know well. Ali also seemed to be in charge of security but that is another story. I stood at the immigration desk (a table) while Ali who could read a little English scrutinised my passport and Tanzanian visa, he gave me a small piece of paper which he tore from a plain yellow sheet. I then moved to another table marked 'health'. Ali followed me and after studying my international certificate of vaccination gave me another small piece of plain paper, pink this time.

Good I thought 'that wasn't too bad' and I made for the door marked 'exit'. Ali followed. At the door he took the yellow and pink pieces of paper from me and put them in the waste basket. 'Welcome to Zanzibar' he said in excellent English. 'I have instructions to take your passport to the Ministry for safe keeping'. Fortunately I had been well-briefed by Jerry (never ever part with your passport). I insisted that it should be placed in the safe at the Bwawani Hotel, and after some argument Ali relented and we emerged from the airport to find a government car waiting to take us to the island's only reasonable hotel. The food at the hotel was appalling with one exception, there was an abundance of lobster, crawfish, and prawns the size of rattle snakes. As lobster was the cheapest thing on the nightly menu I survived on this!

The visit was timed to coincide with the arrival of the vessel carrying the new fire engines and sure enough next morning as we stood on the waterfront in Zanzibar town the 'City of Winchester' appeared on the horizon and eventually anchored in the bay - it was much too large a vessel to get into the tiny port. The excited 'firemen', some bedraggled looking dock workers, Jerry and me, armed with the relevant paperwork, set off for the ship in the only serviceable lighter. On board the ship Captain Dhor invited Jerry and myself to his cabin for a delicious meal of fillet steak accompanied by fresh vegetables from his on deck garden and accompanied by ice-cold

Boddington's beer. He then broke the bad news. A bulldozer going to Durban had broken loose in the hold during a storm and badly damaged four of the fire engines. Because all cargo destined for Tanzania (Zanzibar although proclaiming to be independent is technically part of Tanzania) is covered by state rather than private marine insurance, they would have to be unloaded - he could not take them back to the UK. Our problems were just beginning.

One at a time the fire appliances and ambulances were loaded on to the lighter by the ships derricks and ferried to the quayside. There the only crane in working order was for loads up to 5 tons, the WRT's and the ET's fully laden weighed over 7 tons and every time a lift was attempted the overload tilt alarm bell sounded. The operator would jump from the cabin shouting obscenities in broken English, Swahili and Arabic. I had every confidence in the crane purely because it was built in Birmingham in 1912. Cranes built in Birmingham don't fall over. A handful of Tanzanian shillings for each lift had the miraculous effect of making the operator stone deaf, ensuring that he did not hear the alarm bell! The crane made horrible noises but the unloading was completed without mishap.

It took all day to unload the machines and ferry them up to the airport, which I would use as a base and as it had the only serviceable fire hydrant on the island I would use it for most of the training. It took another day to build them up from their export pack, but it was during this process we discovered another problem. When we opened the lockers on one of the emergency tenders all the equipment had been stolen. Now this is not at all unusual but in this case the lockers were full of carpets. Evidently, somewhere en route, probably at Mombasa, the local mafia had 'done a deal' believing that the fire engines would be unloaded at Dar-es-Salaam. With all the carpets duly disposed of there was going to be a very angry gang of crooks in Dar-es-Salaam. 'Inshaalah' (god willing) they would not come to Zanzibar.

While working at the airport I used one of the water tenders as transport to and from the hotel, and on the second morning I was happily driving to the airport when as I passed one of the frequent road side checkpoints manned by revolutionary guards. Sitting on a soap box with a rusty rifle, unusually the 'guard' was not asleep. All persons and vehicles except government vehicles have to stop at these checkpoints, the 'guard' would then wake up and wave you on. A fire engine is to my mind a government vehicle and I never bothered to stop at these check points. Suddenly the old Land Rover drives alongside with its siren wailing and an 'officer' is waving a pistol signalling me to stop.

I pulled in but made no attempt to get out of the cab, the scruff with the pistol and lemon curd lapels, along with the guard with the rusty rifle came over to the engine. With both weapons pointing at me orders were shouted, 'Out, out, you no stop, passport, passport'. I didn't hesitate, sweating profusely I climbed out of the cab on to legs that felt like jelly. I explained in a trembling voice that my passport was at the Bwawani Hotel and that a fire engine was a government vehicle. 'That no good! Name, name.' 'My name is Hibbert. I am from England'. There was a pause, then to my amazement the officer booted 'rusty rifle man' in the testicles, and as he doubled up, dropping his rifle, he was promptly kicked again. 'Fool, fool, you bloody fool. This is Mr Heebert!' he screamed and with that he threw his arms round me, his pistol next to my ear. 'I am very very sorry, Mr Heebert, please you no tell Mr Karume.' I can still remember the smell of cordite from his revolver along with his own overpowering bodily stench. At this point I didn't even know who Mr Karume was - but I was to find out that same evening.

At Heathrow Airport on the way out I had bought Frederick Forsyth's

new novel *The Dogs of War* for no other reason than it was listed as the Book of the Month. Frederick Forsyth novels are incredibly accurate; his history and location research is to the finest detail. I sat at the bar of the Bwawani Hotel the night of the gun incident reading *The Dogs of War* in-between watching the nightly entertainment of the staff chasing rats the size of tom cats around the bar and dining room. In chapter three Frederick Forsyth details the evil regime of the dictator of the African country in which the novel is set comparing him to General Amin of Uganda and ex President Kurume of Zanzibar. It goes on to describe how Kurume was shot dead while playing cards in the Bwawani hotel. My hair was already 'standing on end' as I looked up to see only feet away from me bullet holes in the wall and the wooden armchair where Kurume had been sitting when he was assassinated. As I broke into a cold sweat I became aware that I was not alone, a tall and well-dressed black man was standing beside me. 'Good evening Mr Hibbert', he said in excellent English, 'my name is Amani Kurume. I am the minister of transport and communications, I am sorry I could not be here to welcome you when you arrived. My cold sweat turned to a very hot sweat as I hastily tried to hide the book. Amani Kurume, it turned out, was the son of the assassinated president I was reading about. (He is now His Excellency President Amini Kurume)

I had come to Zanzibar to commission new fire engines but before this could even start I had to teach the 'firemen' the very basics, how to run out and make up hose, how to ship a standpipe, holding a branch (jet), how to prime the pump, pump throttle control, how to engage the power take off, high and low pressure modes and many other basics fire fighting procedures. The breathing apparatus sets supplied at great expense were put into storage - there was no possibility of training with these as there was no compressor on the island to recharge the high-pressure compressed air cylinders.

Although in reality I was not in Zanzibar to train firemen it was appreciated, and enjoyed, by all. One young man stood out from the rest, and without his help it would have been impossible. Abdul Ali Malamussey was largely self-educated and he could write as well as speak excellent English. I placed him in charge and was later to recommend to the government that he should receive professional training. He eventually came to England for training at Washington Hall Training School run by Lancashire Fire Brigade there he won a place to study at the world fire service technical college at

Moreton-in-Marsh. Today he is Director of the Tanzanian fire service. The emergency services on Zanzibar are far different today and I am proud of the part I played. Ali Malamussey and I are still in touch 30 years later.

The chief of police and government officials were very impressed with the progress we made and it appeared to them that they had acquired a modern workable fire service 'overnight'. The reality was somewhat different. I was asked that if there was an outbreak of fire while I was on the island would I take charge and respond with a crew and one of the new engines. I must admit I was flattered but I did not contemplate that three days later this would happen.

For 'open water' pump training we used the sea water creek at the back of the Bwawani Hotel where we got three jets 'to work' to try and wash years of seagull droppings off the statue of ex President Kurume. I did not even think that had the statue broken I may never have been seen again. It was during one of these pumping sessions that a policeman arrived in a fluster with information that there was a fire in a coconut plantation near Mahonda that was threatening a village.

I instructed Ali Malamussey to pick four men to sit in the crew compartment of the WRT, he would sit in the front with me and I would drive, the rest of the men should 'make up' the hoses and equipment and follow on in the Land Rovers with Micky Daddy in charge. What happened was utter undisciplined chaos, in their enthusiastic excitement ten men climbed into the back of the WRT and about another ten climbed onto the roof. As we set off down a dirt road with siren wailing and Ali giving me directions I was thoroughly enjoying myself as cattle-drawn carts, pedestrians and the odd cyclists fled from the road. I did not know that there were men on the roof, and most of these were knocked off by the overhanging bushes and palm trees. Fortunately the only injuries were a broken leg, one broken arm and many cuts and bruises.

When we arrived at the fire, now only yards from some straw huts, I got two hose reels to work and left Ali Malamussey to organise the rest of the crew with beaters and spades. In spite of some apparent reluctance on their part to tackle the fire it was quickly under control and out in about half an hour, and wearing shorts and pumps I did an inspection of the burned under growth and emerged very dirty just as a government car arrived. Mr Kurume and two other government officials stepped out. My hand was shaken many times and I was told what a fine example I had set to the firemen by not being afraid of the boom-slangs. I had never heard of a boom-slang but was to learn that they are small snakes that live in trees and when disturbed they take umbrage and drop onto unsuspecting victims. Their bite is fatal.

The full significance of this was to hit me many months later while in South Africa when I obtained a snake chart; the advice and information for the boom-slang read: 'Their bite is

BOOM-SLANG
(Dispholdius typus)

TREATMENT As the polyvalent antivenin does not neutralise the venom of this species, the monovalent Boomslang antivenin must be used. This antivenin is not generally available but is obtainable in confirmed cases of poisoning from the South African Institute for Medical Research, Johannesburg. Transfusions of whole blood will be very necessary to replace that being continually lost, and should be repeated until prothrombin time improves.

nearly always fatal, the venom has a serious haemotoxic action....' The standard snake polyvalent snake antivenin does not neutralise the venom of this species and the monovalent boom slang antivenin must be used, only available from the South African Medical Research Centre in Johannesburg. Transfusions of whole blood will be very necessary to replace that being continually lost'. To put it more simply with the only treatment thousands of miles away, had I encountered an angry boom-slang in Zanzibar the British High Commission would have had the job of getting my body back to England.

I returned to Zanzibar some months later following many requests to the CFE for Mr Hibbert to carry out more training and to try to sort out the problem of getting the damaged machines repaired. In spite of long, complex, and frustrating negotiations with the Tanzanian state insurance company that I was involved in long after CFE had closed, there was little progress. With the exception of some repair work that I carried out, the worst damaged machines were eventually cannibalised for spares.

It was while leaving Zanzibar for the last time that I found that my friend Ali at the airport had taken delivery of a new walk through metal detecting security arch, of which he was very proud. By now I was a familiar sight at the airport and handshakes had long since replaced any sort of procedure. My chartered Cessna arrived on time at 7am and I said my farewells and walked out onto the concrete apron to the plane.

With my luggage on board I was just about to climb into the seat alongside the pilot when Ali came running towards the plane shouting 'Mr. Hibbert come back, you must come back' my heart dropped for I had not told the government when I was leaving (it was always wise not to). Should I make a dash for it - or return to the terminal building? I reluctantly chose the latter and with Ali at my side walked back in the morning heat to the tiny terminal building. 'Mr Heebbert you have not been through security machine'! 'But Ali,' I explained, 'I am on my own.' 'That does not matter Mr Heebbert; the regulations say that everyone has to go through the new detector.' I felt relieved and smiled as I passed through the new metal detecting arch, but it was than that I noticed that it was not plugged into the wall point. I pointed this out to Ali, 'for you Mr Heebbert it does not matter, the regulations do not say that it has to be plugged in, and anyway we have no electricity this morning'. I loved Zanzibar and 28 years later I still communicate with Ali Abdul Malamussy.

I arrived in Dar-es-Salaam en route to Arusha to repair the hose reel pump on a Bedford WRT to find that the internal Air Tanzanian flight I was booked on to Kilimanjaro had not operated for months. This was serious as the only two reasonable hotels were full and you do not hang about in darkened streets in Africa. After a prolonged rugby scrum I managed to get booked on a flight the following day, as did a party of German tourists. The problem was that as is the norm on internal African flights, it was already triple booked. I spent the night as the only white man in a dirty run down hotel; I didn't get undressed nor did I sleep, and the crack of dawn saw me at the airport where there was already an unruly queue for the flight in five hours time. It was absolute bedlam as I fought my way to the check-in desk and with the aid of an airport policeman I had 'slipped' some US dollars to, obtained a boarding pass.

When the ageing BA-111 drew up in front of the terminal building there was a mad dash to it even before it had stopped (another normal practice on African internal flights), and after the fight up the steps I got a seat next to a man with a crate of chickens on his knee. The smell from the chickens helped to neutralise my own smell! I hadn't had a wash or changed any clothes for over 48 hours and in the African heat that doesn't do a lot for your charisma. A message came over the tannoy in English and Swahili 'Would passengers in the first ten rows come on to the tarmac to identify their luggage.' I did not move - if you got off you did not get back on. The procedure is repeated until enough room is found for the people standing in the aisles; you just hope and pray that your luggage is on board. The German tourists were foolish enough to get off and were left shouting on the tarmac when the plane eventually taxied for take off.

On the flight to Kilimanjaro, which took an hour, we had the luxury of in-flight refreshments - a boiled sweet. On arrival I boarded an overcrowded bus for Arusha getting off at the Mount Meru Hotel. Arusha is the tourist centre for the Serengeti and on the way we passed herds of wildebeest. The hotel was luxury compared with the last two weeks and at last I was able to take a bath. Two days later, with the repairs I was there for completed, I took a taxi back to Kilimanjaro to catch the British Airways flight back to London. Passing a green mamba sunning itself in the road, I asked the taxi driver to stop while I took a photograph but the terrified driver was having nothing do to with this mad Englishman and put his foot down. The Super VC 10 arrived from Dar-es-Salaam on time, and when airborne it was heaven to be offered champagne, smoked salmon and coffee with Devon cream.

But the adventures of this trip were not yet over. After flying over Lake Victoria, the Aswan Dam and following the River Nile to the sea we should have landed in Cyprus at Larnaca for refuelling, but the pilot made three hairy attempts to land in thick fog before diverting to Athens. On arrival in the early hours coaches were waiting to take all the passengers and crew to the luxurious Appalon Palace Hotel, because with the crew 'out of time' we were to stay here for twenty-four hours, situated next to the beach, with a coach tour of Athens and a visit to the Acropolis laid on, top quality food, free drinks and phone calls. It was well worth the disappointment of arriving home a day late. Well done, British Airways.

Zanzibar is a beautiful and unspoiled island with lovely people... and I should add that it now has first class hotels and is well worth visiting.

Abdul, Abdul, Abdullah, Abdul and Jerry with City of Winchester in background

Lighter crew with turtle shells in Zanzibar port.

Unloading the new fire engines at Zanzibar.

Fire crews training alongside the statue of President Kurume.

The young firemen were delighted with their new fire engines.

'...in their enthusiastic excitement ten men climbed into the back of the WRT...' page 63

Crash tender, Zanzibar airport!

Bwawani Hotel from the bay.

One of the houses threatened by the plantation fire.

My first sight of Mount Kilimanjaro

HOUSE OF COMMONS
LONDON SWIA OAA   27th May 1980

Dear Mr Hibbert,

I read with interest the article about you in last week's Macclesfield Express. I congratulate ERF on winning an order from Zanzibar worth over one million pounds ed I wish you success and good fortune during your imminent visit to Zanzibar when you will be demonstrating fire fighting techniques. I would like to take this opportunity of thanking you

Letter from Nicholas Winterton M.P.

CHAPTER VIII
SWAZILAND

The most stable country in Africa, in recent history, is the Kingdom of Swaziland, and with the exception of the invasion by Michael Caine and the film crews to make the epic 'Zulu' there has never been a war in Swaziland, Zulu was filmed in the beautiful Ezulwini valley where Rider Haggard wrote *King Solomon's Mines*, and the film employed hundreds of local Zulus as extras. The pinnacle shaped rock that is seen in the battle scenes is actually called Execution Rock.

You might think that Michael Caine and his fellow actors had to 'rough it' in this apparent wilderness - not a bit. What you don't see in the film, one mile behind the cameras, is an 18-hole championship golf course, the famous Royal Casino with its sauna and hot springs, a Holiday Inn, swimming pools, the Smokey Mountain Village 'British Pub' and the famous Churchill's bar, renowned for its cocktails.

During the apartheid years gambling in South Africa was illegal, as was mixed race sex, but there were no such restrictions in Swaziland, Botswana, Lesotho (formally Basutoland) and Bophuthatswana - where Sun City was created and designed by South Africa to consolidate apartheid. At weekends and national holidays white South Africans (Afrikaans) would cross the borders to play golf and to visit the casinos and the girls!

His Majesty King Sobhuza II ruled Swaziland and to coincide with his diamond jubilee celebrations on September 4th 1981 the British government through the Overseas Development Agency and Crown Agents funded a new crash tender for Matsapa airport. It was to be delivered and commissioned in time for the arrival of the heads of states from all over the world. The King, who had 100 wives and over 600 children, was a close and personal friend of Princess Margaret and he invited her to represent the United Kingdom.

The new crash tender would effectively upgrade the airport; it would carry 1000 gallons of water and 250 gallons of foam compound; mixed together at high pressure this would enable the roof-mounted cannon to throw thousands of gallons of foam per minute onto an aircraft. CFE won the contract, and it was built on a Shelvoke and Drewery 20 ton chassis along,

AN ADVENTURE IN AFRICA

Graham's race against time and crocodiles

CHESHIRE Fire Engineering employee Graham Hibbert has returned home after a triumphant race against time across 450 miles of sometimes gruelling African terrain.

Mr Hibbert managed to drive a huge 27-ton fire engine from Durban to Swaziland in time for a big royal celebration — attended by Princess Margaret and a host of VIPs.

Swaziland's only airport, at Matsapa, wanted its new fire engine — built by the Winsford firm of Cheshire Fire Engineering — delivered in time for the diamond jubilee celebrations of King Sobhuza, the country's sovereign.

Because of shipping delays, Mr Hibbert, the firm's quality control engineer, was left with a tough deadline to beat . . . and miles of unmade roads and crocodile-infested rivers ahead of him.

Mr Hibbert was aided by three fire officers and had another fire engine in front as an escort.

with a Bedford 4x4 water tender and a Bedford water carrier.

At the end of October the vehicles for the Swaziland Fire Service arrived in Durban, the nearest port to the land-locked country, and the original plan was to transport the vehicles by rail to the Swaziland capital Mmabane. But this meant a long track inland to Germiston, up to Pretoria and then west into war-torn Mozambique before coming east again into Swaziland. This was considered too risky and lengthy, and there was the additional risk that bandits in Mozambique frequently attacked trains. With only three days in which to get the crash tender into service it was decided that I would drive the beast 600 kilometres from Durban, through Natal province, Zululand and into Swaziland at the Big Bend border. It was the shortest but most difficult route using long stretches of dirt roads - to stick with tarmac roads would have taken an extra two days.

After a British Airways 747 from London to Johannesburg I took the internal South African Airways flight to Durban. As we approached Durban I could see what appeared to be thousands of blue patches on the ground, and as we got lower the blue patches turned into swimming pools - it appeared that every house had a swimming pool in their garden. I checked in the Ellengani International Hotel and met up with Nigel Fenwick an ex-Hertfordshire fire officer who was now chief fire officer of Swaziland. Nigel had brought two of his staff with him and next day after collecting the two fire engines and the crash tender from the port we would drive to Swaziland in convoy.

Following a short rest we all met in the bar before a walk on the promenade. Durban is a beautiful city with miles of golden beaches with huge breakers rolling in off the Indian Ocean and providing excellent surfing - when the shark patrols give the 'all clear'. We walked onto the beach, determined to get my feet wet in the clear blue water, but it was at this point that I was to understand the meaning of apartheid. One of Nigel's staff was black and while we walked on the beach he had to stay on the promenade footpath, it was a whites only beach, a smaller inferior beach on the outskirts of town was allocated for blacks.

Next morning at breakfast I was to make a big mistake, 'would Sir like a Continental, English or South African breakfast?' When in Rome! 'South African please'. It was enormous, three eggs, gammon, two sausages, two lamb cutlets, fillet steak, two huge prawns in their shells, hash browns, mushrooms, baked beans and tomatoes, served on a huge oval plate the size of a dinner tray. 'Would Sir like a beer?' 'No Sir would not'. I suppose it was very impolite but I watched in awe as a party of Australians (as I was to witness again in Hong Kong) not only managed to eat the huge breakfast but washed it down with copious quantities of lager. I only managed two eggs, the steak, the prawns, one cutlet, one sausage, and a bit of the gammon before jibbing - and I was to feel stuffed for days.

After some delay with customs we set off north on the coast road, Nigel and I took the lead in the crash tender with its power steering, Allison automatic gearbox and large Perkins diesel engine it was a joy to drive and with no water or foam in the tanks it went 'like a bomb'. The only problem was its width, and the central driving position made judgement quite difficult, a slight lack of concentration would see you drift over the crown of the road. South African armoured army vehicles travelling in the opposite direction were a menace, they had no respect for anything else on the road and they would frequently collide with other vehicles forcing them off the road, and unless the victim was white they would never stop. It was dark when we reached the Mtabatuba Safari Motel in a the national game park near to Rorkes Drift, and after a good dinner and a few beers I retired to find a large green praying mantis on the bed rail. I promptly dispatched it with a book only to be told next morning that praying mantis are harmless and killing them brings bad luck!

Following the essential African morning routine of checking your shoes for overnight lodgers such as scorpions, ants, cockroaches, sand lizards etc I joined the rest of the team for an early breakfast. With half of yesterday's breakfast still undigested I opted for fruit, toast and several coffees. We set off early and soon reached the South African/Swaziland border where at the tiny border post the South African police were completely out of their depth and had no idea how to document three bright yellow fire engines. After a little financial persuasion in the time honoured way the border police miraculously decided that there was no need for any documentation and we were allowed to pass into 'no mans land', a quarter of a mile up the road at the Swaziland post there were no problems, they were expecting us, they knew Nigel and we received a warm welcome.

We were on unmade roads now and the rest of the day would be rough going with several narrow bridges of doubtful weight capacity. From the border at Big Bend - there is no bend at Big Bend! -the road is straight for about forty miles but at that time of year the road dusty and corrugated. Corrugated road surfaces could wreck a vehicle in a very short space of time, and the secret was to ride the corrugations by driving at speed so that the tyres literally bounced off the top of each ridge; the speed, usually around 50mph, varied according to the vehicles wheelbase and was arrived at by trial and error. Unfortunately I could not find the optimum speed for the crash tender because of the dust clouds reducing visibility to almost zero at times, and the shaking was horrendous. The vehicle took a severe pounding, and this was to have dire consequences in a month's time. I definitely should not have killed that praying mantis!

The next serious obstacles were a number of single track bridges. One in particular was just slab concrete with no sides, there was just three inches to spare each side before a 12 foot drop into a crocodile infested river - three inches might sound quite a lot but the huge wheels on the crash tender meant that you could be at the edge in seconds. Heart in mouth, soaked in sweat and wondering if the spirits of the dead praying mantis were willing me into the river, I had a guide walking backwards in front of me and I slowly inched the 20 ton machine over the 10 ton weight limit bridge. When we reached safety I climbed out of the cab on to weak knees and much to the amusement of the native onlookers we all spontaneously cheered. Later when CFE issued a press release, a photograph of this epic river crossing appeared in several newspapers.

After several more difficult and rough stretches we were back on tarmac roads and made Mmabane by nightfall. I was booked in at the Swazi Inn, not far from the Royal Palace and as I was to discover the next day that it would also be used by some of Princess Margaret's entourage. That evening at the bar the beer tasted particularly good and with J&B, my favourite blended whisky inexpensive, I slept like a log.

The next morning I drove the crash tender to the airport and began to familiarise the airport fire crews with its operation, hopefully in time for the arrival of the aircraft carrying heads of state and VIPs later in the day. Half a day isn't much time to learn how to operate a complex fire crash tender. Fortunately unlike firemen in some parts of Africa the Swazi men were professional, disciplined, and many of them had been to the British Airports Authority fire training school at Teeside airport. Led by the airport's chief

From Bollington to Zanzibar

At Matsapa Airport.

A bridge too far?

Whites only beach
Durban 1981.

Walking to the King's
Jubilee celebrations.

fire officer, ex-English fire officer Colin Reeves, they were a great crew to work with. There were good water and foam supplies and we soon had the unit operational, so that when the RAF Royal Fight Andover, carrying Princess Margaret, arrived thirty minutes early I was manning the foam cannon. A short while later I witnessed one of those things you never see on television - during a short gap in the red carpet welcomes and inspections, the guard of honour who had been standing in file for several hours, suddenly broke rank, ran to the perimeter fence and all urinated together with military precision, before quickly lining up again for the arrival of the next head of state. I believe Princess Margaret was just out of sight behind a flight shed.

Back at the hotel I was asked if I would mind sharing my twin-bedded en suite 'round-house' room with Princess Margaret's hairdresser. Two hours later I was back in reception demanding another room, the hairdresser's sexual preferences were evident, and after a lot of argument I got my room back. They hoisted him onto some other unlucky guest (perhaps lucky, you never know!) Later that evening the Royal Swazi Flying Club hosted a formal dinner for the British Royal Flight crew to which I was invited along with Colin Reeves and Nigel Fenwick. Just my luck; that preying mantis again I thought, as I took my allocated seat I was next to a catholic priest. This is going to be a right boring evening I thought. But my misgivings were unjustified; the priest could put his wine away and was great company. He was on his first posting after completing theological training at Shrigley Hall, the Silesian Missionary college near to my home. Only days earlier we had both been in the Masonic Arms in Bollington - what a coincidence!

The following day was a day off; I was taken to some of Swaziland's stunning locations and purchased a beautiful handmade clock at Copperland's. The clock which I value dearly hangs in our lounge and has always kept perfect time. In the evening we went to the casino where I won two hundred lilangeni on the fruit machine! The lilangeni is roughly equivalent to one rand, and a one lilangeni coin is the same size and weight as a pound coin and at that time was worth about sixty pence. The Swazi currency notes are rather unique in that they depict bare-breasted virgins - some of the king's many daughters!

I left Swaziland with as much South African wine as I could carry and feeling very satisfied. But I would return very shortly and the praying mantis would have its revenge.

Three weeks later a telex arrived at CFE to say that serious weld cracks had been found in the aluminium body framework of the crash tender, the commercial attaché at the British Consulate and the head of engineering at Crown Agents had been informed and the unit taken out of service. It isn't everyday that a £100,000 gift from the British Government is effectively useless after only three weeks in service. Although I was not responsible for the design, nor had I personally carried out the welding inspections as head of quality control the buck stopped with me and I was in a lot of trouble. 'On the carpet' in the managing director's office I was instructed to get the crash tender back into service as quickly as possible with the minimal of political flack; the consequences of this incident had the potential to damage British engineering exports. I knew exactly what had caused the damage of course, the terrible pounding inflicted by the hours of driving on corrugations and one dead praying mantis, but I did not think the CFE management would have been impressed with either excuse. Within 24 hours I was back on a flight back to Swaziland via Johannesburg.

On arrival I accessed the damage and promised the British High Commissioner 'tongue in cheek' that I would have the unit back in service within one week. There were no local facilities for aluminium welding so I telexed CFE ordering 150 angle gussets. They were to work through the night manufacturing them and to fly them out along with 600 8mm high tension set bolts and lock nuts along with other fittings, tools with a fitter the following day. I met Keith the fitter/bodybuilder at the airport and we worked twelve hours in sweltering heat without a break and had the crash tender back in service with a stronger body two days later. A diplomatic and financially embarrassing incident had been averted but CFE's quality reputation had been damaged.

On the way home while driving back to Johannesburg I had the misfortune to be searched at the South African border post by a very stroppy black police team. I had to spread all the contents of my suitcase in the road including the many bottles of wine wrapped up in my dirty washing. At this point I promised never to kill anything larger than a fly again in my life! The borders guards were looking for fruit - because of the fear of spreading disease to the pineapple crop it is illegal to carry fruit across the border. But eventually they allowed me and my black driver to continue on our way. And once again in South Africa stopping for refreshments was always a problem

- we had to find two cafés, one for whites and one for blacks.

With rumours rife that ERF were about to close CFE, I thought this would to be my last visit to Africa. But it was not, and in three years time I would come close to 'meeting my end' in Nigeria. The company's Swazi agent was Adrian Sharp and between us we had discussed an idea to build modular ambulances in kit form to be assembled in Swaziland. While this was a dream that never materialised it was the basis of an idea that enabled me, following the closure of CFE, to start a new career with a new company which would lead to new horizons and new adventures.

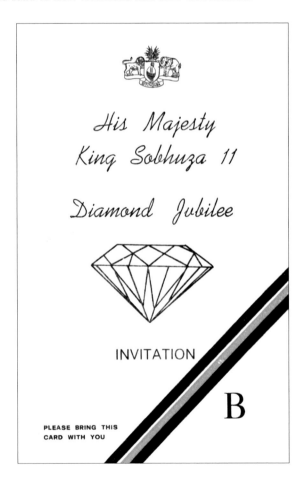

His Majesty
King Sobhuza 11

Diamond Jubilee

INVITATION

B

PLEASE BRING THIS
CARD WITH YOU

Guard of honour and welcoming party for Princess Margaret.

Fully operational, just in time for the Princess's arrival.

Brunei sunset.

CHAPTER IX
DOWN UNDER - A NEW BEGINNING

It was with mixed feelings that I tidied my desk for the last time before leaving Cheshire Fire Engineering. I was one of the last staff to leave and only sub-contractors were left in the huge factory. Relief from the heavy responsibility was my main emotion - followed by concern for my future. I had never been made redundant before nor had I ever been out of work but at least the weeks of rumours were now over. Finance was not an immediate problem, the redundancy pay and the union negotiated severance settlement was generous, and there was always my fire service earnings to fall back on. Never for one moment did I consider I might have to go on the dole.

Ten days later I started work at a former CFE sub-contractor, Macclesfield Motor Bodies. My job was vague to say the least but I had obviously impressed MMB's owner and managing director Ian Woolhouse with my 'tongue in cheek' promises that I could secure lucrative fire engine repair work and export ambulance contracts. In hindsight this was an ambitious goal considering that no one at MMB, a car repair company, knew anything about fire engines or ambulances, let alone how to design them.

Three incredible strokes of luck would shape the next twenty years of my life. The first was the free hand and the backing afforded me by Ian Woolhouse. The second was a chance meeting with Arthur Jones, an ex Herbert Lomas foreman, who without hesitation I enlisted as my first 'employee'. Arthur was a truly remarkable man, a master craftsman and tradesman of the highest calibre; without doubt one of England's finest. Arthur had a superbly inventive mind that he could put into practice. He also had an in depth knowledge of ambulances. My third stroke of luck, was acquiring Mary O'Toole as my secretary and assistant. Mary had an engineering background - and the remarkable ability of being able to read my writing! In addition to her management skills Mary is extremely good looking, Without the help of Mary and Arthur MMB International would not have been born and certainly would not be the successful company that it is today. Mary is now the manager of MMB International.

In the early weeks and months there was a lot of canvassing and cold sales-calling to be done proclaiming the expertise and quality of a company that in reality did not exist. It was very much a 'chicken and egg' bluff scenario but eventually I got a fire engine repair and maintenance contract from Hestair Dennis and an ambulance order from MWG Ltd, a Surrey based vehicle exporting company. MMB Special Vehicles Ltd was born.

At least once a month I would visit Crown Agents in London. The Crown Agents were then a thriving organisation looking after the whole of the British Commonwealth and occupying an imposing building on the Thames Embankment close to the Houses of Parliament. Catching the 06.50 train from Macclesfield to London I could be in Alan Holdaway's office by 09.30. Alan was responsible for the purchase of vehicles including ambulances and a friendly but professional relationship was built up that was to last for many years and would result in orders for many commonwealth countries.

A Crown Agent's order for two Ford Transit ambulances for Sabah, coincided with a contract from Carmichael Fire Ltd to build four V.W. rescue ambulances for the Brunei Fire Service. As part of the contract Carmichael's would pay me to commission their fire engines as well as the ambulance vehicles, with Sabah only a 50-minute flight from Bandar Seri Begawan the Brunei capital and the delivery of the Sabah ambulances conveniently coinciding I was able to combine the two.

Brunei is close to Sarawak, Borneo and Sabah. It is north of Australia in the Celebes Sea and this was the nearest I ever got to Australia. Sixteen hours after leaving London the British Airways 747 flight to Perth landed in Bandar Seri Begawan where Carmichael's agent met me. Brunei - or to give its correct name Negara Brunei Darussalam - came somewhat as a shock and was a world apart from the poverty and chaos of Africa. A quick tour of the airport's well-equipped emergency services made me realise I would be dealing with well-trained professionals and my job would not be easy - in a completely different context to previous commissioning.

After checking in at the Sheraton Utama I settled down to two days in five star luxury before starting work. Warm swimming pools, jacuzzis, best New Zealand steaks, local lobster, good beer and wine - and an unlimited budget - it was the start of a 'good life' that I was to enjoy many times in the next twenty years.

Brunei is a Sultanate ruled by the world's richest man, His Majesty Sultan Haji Hassanal Bolkiah Muizzaddi Waddaulah, the Sultan and Yang Di-Pertuan of Brunei Darrussalam. A newsreader's nightmare! He is a good friend of Britain and the British Royal Family, and in addition to oil fields, Brunei has some of the world's most beautiful palaces. The Sultan also owns a large part of central London. The 28,000 Brunei nationals enjoy the highest per capita income in the world, the oil fields produce in excess of 160,000 barrels per day, and it has the largest liquefied gas field in the world. The religion is a form of Islam, Malayu Islam Beraja.

Whenever the Sultan or his family leave the royal palace they are accompanied by a police escort with wailing sirens, and this seemed to happen several times a day during my stay. It was fascinating to watch people and traffic come to a standstill until the royal motorcade had swept past.

The modern fire stations, training facilities and high standard of education made my job easy, and with the exception of hydraulic problems with the crash rescue equipment all went smoothly. My task was completed in four days - with English being the predominant language, communication was not a problem. In fact as you will read later out of 48 countries I have visited worldwide, only in France did I find that people did not speak English.

With Carmichael's commissioning in Brunei completed it was time to 'wear my own company's hat' and move on to Sabah. I boarded a Royal Brunei Airline 737 for Kota Kinabulu, to find I was the only white person on board. The hour-long flight was made in an horrendous thunderstorm with the plane subjected to frightening turbulence. The Malay cabin crew were very good, tightening seat belts, handing out sick bags and comforting passengers. I remember thinking I hope the pilot knows what he's doing. I had memories of news flashes after a plane crash in an obscure country, to the effect that 'the Foreign Office has confirmed that there was one British national on board', and I would be asking myself what on earth were they doing there? I don't mind a bit of turbulence but it is when you drop several thousand feet at a time and you have to concentrate your mind on bowel control that you cease to enjoy the flight. After 50 minutes the skies cleared and it became a little less bumpy, and at this point there was an announcement from the flight deck that made it an unforgettable flight. In a broad Yorkshire dialect it went, 'Good Morning ladies and gentlemen, this is your captain, Cyril Arkwright speaking. Sorry for th' bumpy ride, we will shortly be landing at Kota Kinabalu, thanks for flying Royal Brunei and we hope to see thee again sometime.' I suddenly felt much better.

Sabah's chief fire officer was waiting for me at the airport and several more days of luxury followed at the Tringe Beach Hotel. Sabah is about half way between Australia and Japan, and a favourite meeting place for businessmen visiting the Mount Kinabulu national park. The poolside service is outstanding, when lazing in the jacuzzi you had only to glance in the direction of the bar and an ice cold Australian lager would be in your hand in seconds.

One of the benefits of a business class open ticket is that you can change flights, airlines and even routes. It was Friday and the following day Elsie and I were supposed to be going to a fire service dance in Bollington. The original plan was to fly back to Brunei and catch the BA flight to Heathrow on Sunday but after browsing timetables at the Malaysian Air office in Kota Kinabulu I decided to take the MAS evening flight to Singapore, a KLM flight to Amsterdam via New Dehli and finally a BA flight to Manchester. I arrived home late Saturday afternoon tired and jet lagged - but we made the dance.

Royal Brunei and MAS are excellent airlines unlike KLM which I would not recommend - this leg was long and not enjoyable. The transit stop at Singapore's new futuristic Changi airport was nostalgic for me, with its indoor gardens and waterfalls it must be one of the most beautiful in the world. It is built on the very location of the notorious Japanese army prison, and later the British army transit camp that I had stayed in 30 years previously.

CHAPTER X
UNITED ARAB EMIRATES

My first of many visits to the UAE like many of my overseas sales 'jollies' was with a government subsidised trade mission and was concentrated on Dubai and Oman. Subsequent visits included Bahrain, Qatar and Abu Dhabi.

Trade mission flights were always in economy class, not the most comfortable long haul travel particularly if you were sat next to some foreign nationals. On one Gulf Air Bahrain-London flight I witnessed two men urinate in the aisle and a mother stand a boy on to the seat while he urinated into a cushion. Virtually all Arab business men would travel business or first class and later thanks mainly to my daughter's capacity as public relations manager at Manchester Airport I used to get upgraded to business or first class. First class air travel with the world's leading airlines is absolute pampered luxury, with menus comparable to leading restaurants, the very best smoked salmon, caviar and steaks all served on the finest Staffordshire pottery, with the best champagne, malt whisky, cognac and wines. Seating is the height of comfort with always enough space to lie flat and tables that swing back to enable you to go to the loo without disturbing your meal. Your personal fold-away entertainment screen offers a choice all the latest films. The flower arrangements are renewed throughout the flight. It is not difficult to understand that when money 'is no object' why the world's rich and famous pay thousands of pounds extra to travel first class.

On my first visit to Dubai I met up with Nick Youdon of Land Rover at the Intercontinental Hotel, close to the airport. Nick and I were good friends, he knew Dubai well and offered to take me for dinner. This was an opportunity not to be missed as Nick was not usually known for dipping in to his 'expenses'. We took the hotel courtesy minibus to town and dined at the famous Camel restaurant, the 'eat as much as you like' Indian buffet was ideal for Nick's ferocious appetite. I'm not a lover of Indian food but washed down with a few beers it wasn't too bad.

It was a warm moonlit night and Nick in his wisdom decided we would walk back to the hotel. After an hour he had to admit we were hopelessly lost, we could hear the airport and see the high level navigation lights over the top of the palm trees on the other side of the dual carriageway but it was dark on an unlit road in a foreign country and I was tired. 'Come on Nick get a taxi and I'll buy you a pint of draught beer in John Smith's bar when we get back', Reluctantly Nick flagged down a passing taxi and was immediately involved in some sort of argument with the driver; our Arabic was not good but we agreed to pay ten dinars, a relatively small amount. We got into the taxi travelled a hundred yards down the dual carriageway, round a roundabout and back a hundred yards to the entrance to the hotel. The driver had been trying to tell us we had only to cross the road and no doubt thought us completely mad. Needless to say in addition to the pint of John Smith's beer Nick got a lot of ribbing - and still does. Incidentally fish, chips and mushy peas in John Smith's in Dubai are as good as those in Whitby.

Dubai has the cheapest and best duty free shop in the world, the centre piece being a top of the range car usually a BMW or Mercedes car that is raffled weekly, and the car is shipped to any part of the world. From the water front 'creek' dhows ferry goods all over the Gulf, everything from TV sets, computers, fridges and cars are stacked up on the open quay with no guards or security. Even in the gold Suike there seemed very little security, no one steals in Dubai - the cutting off of a thief's hand must be a very good deterrent.

The UAE has some of the most beautiful and luxurious hotels in the world; among these is the Al Bustan Palace hotel in Oman and the Sheraton Doha in Qatar. Muscat, the capital of Oman, is an hour's flight from Dubai. Oman is a beautiful country with virtually no crime; even speeding can get you a prison sentence. My first entry to Oman was somewhat dramatic. At Muscat airport I stood in a queue at immigration for over two hours in sweltering heat waiting to get my CNO (Certificate of No Objection). The man in front of me was arrested and led away screaming and objecting. But I need not have worried, I had an English passport and was treated with the utmost courtesy, and after twenty minutes interrogation my passport was duly stamped and the CNO issued. I think we have a lot to learn about immigration control in this country.

It was now 3.00am as the hotel minibus made its way to Muttrah on the outskirts of Muscat. In the centre of the dual carriageway, miles of rose beds were in full bloom. In places the road passed old forts and went through dramatic rock cuttings, with animals such as Ibex sculptured on the rock face and waterfalls cascading down the gullies. The animals, buildings and waterfalls were all floodlit in spectacular colours. Rose gardens and waterfalls in a land where it rarely rains? Water is pumped from the sea to create the falls and then it is desalinated for watering the gardens. The Sultan had decreed that Oman should be beautiful and it truly was - and I had yet to see it in daylight.

At the Al Bustan Palace Hotel there were guards everywhere all armed to the teeth with machete like swords, pistols and Kalashnikov rifles. In the morning I would learn that Margaret Thatcher was staying in the Sultan's penthouse suite that occupied the whole of the top floor, and all guests were confined to the hotel lobby whenever she and her massive police escort was about - I would miss a business appointment later in the week due to this, which was extremely annoying.

Next morning was a day off, and the hotel gardens and pool were next to what must be the loveliest beach in the world, golden pure sand sloping gently to a crystal clear warm sea where multi-coloured fish swim around you. The poolside bar and barbeque served British beer, Australian lager, succulent steaks and of course lobster. All this in a country with no brewery, no cows and where alcohol consumption was for non-arabs only. Many of the large ex-patriate community in Muscat use the hotel facilities and enjoy a very good lifestyle. It was very easy to forget I was here to sell ambulances and would be meeting the chief police procurement officer and head of army medical services the following day. Four days later I was back home and planning my next visit to the UAE that would include Bahrain and Qatar.

Bahrain is the cosmopolitan crossroad of the Middle East where rich Arabs drive across the giant causeway from Saudi Arabia in their Cadillacs, to do all the things that they are not allowed to do at home. This includes getting drunk, listening and even dancing to western pop music, and sampling the Philippine girls (or Philippine house boys). I have witnessed huge sums of money, and genuine Rolex watches, thrown on to the stage at the Hilton Hotel when a girl pop group was performing. Each 'gift' would have the donor's hotel room number attached to it. At the respectable international hotels all the money and gifts are collected and donated to charity. A tragedy of this practice is that the Arabs who have probably never drunk alcohol in their lives crash their cars and are killed or injured. My first visit to Bahrain was successful resulting in an order for two Landrover 130 rescue ambulances for the police. When I returned a year later I was amazed

Al Bustan Palace Hotel, Muscat.

to find that the hotel barman remembered me. When my son was in the RAF during the Gulf war a squadron of Tornado pilots had been based at this hotel. Qatar was only a short flight from Bahrain and it had a permanent British Aerospace (BA) presence. BA owned Land Rover and with established lines of credit worth millions of pounds the business opportunities looked good. I arrived at the futuristic Doha Sheraton as usual in the middle of the night. Qatar is a strict Muslim country with severe penalties for drinking alcohol. However the BA office in Muscat had tipped me off that the Sheraton had a special dispensation and one room had been set aside where visitors could get a drink. The problem was it was illegal for the hotel to tell its guests where this facility was. The following day I was determined to find 'the secret room'. Reception was no help but eventually a kindly Australian, seeing the thirsty look on my face, directed me up an internal bubble lift to a mezzanine floor where I passed a security check before entering 'the room'. It was amazing - here was a perfect replica of a Cornish pub complete with lobster pots on the wall, Boddington's bitter, a pool table, a food counter serving roast beef with Yorkshire puddings and Cornish pasties - it was packed with 'ex-pats'. The following day when I met up with the guy from Land Rover who had stayed at the hotel before I said, 'Let's go to the bar for a drink.' 'You can't get a drink in here,' he said. 'You bet, you can!'

Unfortunately after a lot of negotiations, the day before the signing of a contract, BA announced out of the blue it was selling Land Rover, they were no longer a BA company product and the lines of credit were withdrawn. I returned home never to return to Qatar again.

The Doha Sheraton where I found the Cornish pub.

Medical convention in Slovakia.

CHAPTER XI
REFLECTIONS ON EUROPE

Europe with its modern railway systems, low cost air flights (unless you are flying from Manchester to Paris)) and autobahns make its easy to travel. Nearly everyone in Europe except the French speak good English making it a pleasure for business and stress free holidays. But for exporters there is one big problem, Britain is not in the Euro currency zone, a huge disadvantage, especially now that the United Nations only deals in Euros and US dollars. These are some of my observations from travelling around Europe in the 1980s and 1990s.

Poland

Very pro British, the Poles have a warm charm; the things I remember most are the large Cadbury's chocolate factory near Wroclaw and the casinos.

I booked a first class rail ticket from East Berlin to Wroclaw expecting an uncomfortable journey on wooden seats. Yes the train was old but the carriages were the closest thing to the Orient Express you are ever likely to find, and the on-board immigration police unlike those at airports took only a cursory look at my documentation before settling down to their card games.

Republic of Slovakia

Is largely unknown to the British traveller, yet the boundary is only a $^1/_2$ hour drive from Vienna and a further hour before you reach the bridge over the River Danube and the capital Bratislava. It is a relatively safe country to drive around with reasonable hotels, but there are pockets of poverty. The big problem with Slovakia is that it still struggles with a legacy of Eastern European bureaucracy that produces mountains of paperwork to keep people in work - to produce yet more paperwork.

At a health care convention in Banska Bystrica I was given two minutes notice to speak before an audience of doctors at a medical seminar. I managed to speak for twenty minutes on the subject of winter sports injuries and how bad it could be for tourism and their economy if there were not the trained personnel equipped with the best emergency and rescue vehicles (mine of course) to deal with them.

My talk was well received and eventually an order of intent for 50 Land Rover ambulances was received, unfortunately there was no money to pay for them, many years on MMB are still waiting for a confirmed and irrevocable letter of credit before any contract can commence.

France
France is a beautiful country but it has a gigantic problem, the French. They are arrogant, ignorant, insular, greedy, devious, sly, dishonest, selfish, drive like maniacs with a complete disregard for anyone - and that is their good points. They are also blatantly anti-British - although I have been told they are basically anti-everybody. They have the laziest, wealthiest farmers in Europe all supported by EU funds. They break every EC law but expect all other countries to comply, they have ferocious looking female lavatory attendants who always seem to be mopping around your feet and try to charge you five euros for a pee - while outside all the French men piss in the street. In Nice I was chased along the promenade because I had dared to use the urinals without putting the obligatory francs into the bowl, because I had no small change.

And don't ask a French policeman for directions - he will pretend not to speak English (Yes I know that it is their country and I should speak French). In fairness I did find once find a very courteous and helpful young policeman at the Gard de Lyon station.

There's more. The French make excellent wine but sell all their rubbish to the gullible English at Channel port hypermarkets. Their air traffic controllers have a national sport which they play every bank holiday weekend, called 'holiday flight delay'. Not to be out done French fishermen blockade the ports at bank holidays, and while all this is going on, the subsidised French farmers, who are bored stiff with nothing much to do, set fire to English lorries carrying live sheep, and the equally bored French police look on and do nothing. They won't buy our beef but expect us to buy their cheese. A coffee and cognac in Paris or Nice will cost you £9 and a dry ham roll £7.

In case you haven't noticed I don't have a lot time for the French. In Paris they have twelve main roads (boulevards) that converge onto one roundabout that has a lump of concrete in the middle called the Arc de Triomphe. There is no traffic control and no civilised drivers, it is utter madness - it is only a 'triomphe' if you can get round it in one piece.

Should you think I am being just a little unkind towards the French, visit the French pavilion on a trade day at the Farnborough air show and see Exocet missiles for sale. They are proudly marketed as 'battle proven in the Falkland Islands'. Need I say more?

But the French do have a lot to teach us about railways, their TVG trains are superb.

Holland

Without any doubt the Dutch are the friendliest people in Europe, and very pro-British. They are a sincere people, a little too liberal-minded but very professional and honourable in business. I first went to Amsterdam with a contingent of firemen from London (chapter V1) and was amazed to see all the girls in windows. My next visit would be several years later wearing my MMB hat and by then the girls had been largely replaced by boys!

Holland is easy to get around with a good and inexpensive railway system. While visiting a company in Arnhem I took the opportunity to walk over the Rhine bridge and to see the immaculately kept memorials, a very moving experience. I have made some good friends in Holland through my business dealings and I have a great deal of respect for them.

Germany

The many Germans I have had dealings with were efficient, polite and extremely courteous, with an excellent command of English. Not as warm as the Dutch but I experienced no problems whatsoever with the Germans.

Spain

I have never been to Spain on business other than as access to Gibraltar, but like most people I have holidayed there. Given half a chance the taxi drivers will rip you off and the border police at the Gibraltar crossing have a huge attitude problem. Don't expect any service in Spain between midday and 2am, everyone goes to bed for a 'matinee' - known in Spain as a siesta.

Switzerland

My favourite European country. Efficiency comes naturally to the Swiss, trains, buses, lake ferries, cable cars, mountain railways all work to integrated time tables with incredible accuracy. The scenery is stunningly beautiful and many mountains having a restaurant on top with access by cog railway or cable car.

The Swiss never go to war but have an army with national service conscription and they make a lot of money looking after everyone else's money. I think they have probably got it right.

Geneva is the home to the International Red Cross and many United Nations agencies, which resulted in many visits for me, promoting MMB ambulances at the international trade fairs. I was privileged to meet many UK VIP 'ambassadors' on these occasions including the wonderfully enigmatic Terry Waite and the disagreeable Lord David Owen.

The Swiss are liberal and practical, in the station subway under Zurich airport you can see a huge coloured poster depicting a boy and girl lying in a hay field obviously very much in love, the caption reads 'Safe sex, use a condom'. On the opposite platform another poster shows two young men lying in the same hay field and it has the same caption!

Ireland (Eire)
The Irish have a wonderful laid back approach to life and anything that can be put off until tomorrow will be. I first visited Ireland in 1986 to hand over a new £100.000 hydraulic platform to the City of Cork Fire Brigade.(Chapter V1). At MMB we have built several ambulances for the Irish armed forces.

Bulgaria
A £400,000 order for ambulances for the Bulgarian Ministry of Health saw me en route to Sofia. The flight out on a Bulgarian Airways Airbus 300 wasn't too bad but there were no alcoholic drinks and in flight catering left a lot to be desired. At the airport the first call was at the immigration counter where you paid 100 US dollars, cash only, for your visa; entry was then a formality. Holidaymakers don't have to pay for a visa.

The Sheraton Sofia hotel is very good by Eastern European standards with treble locks on the bedroom doors. Crime is rife in Bulgaria, car owners parking their Trapis and Ladas outside their drab apartments remove the wiper blades and wheels and take them inside with them. It was amusing to watch drivers stop to fit the wiper blades when it started to rain. Like many other Eastern bloc countries there is a huge variation in the cars one sees, from totally clapped out bangers to top of the range Mercedes.

One evening during my second visit to Bulgaria I but on my blazer and Land Rover tie and gate-crashed a British Airways promotion dinner at the Sheraton. I claimed I was from Land Rover travel department and was wined and dined in style along with civic dignities and representative of the tourist industry. I was even seen on local television being introduced to civic dignitaries.

The flight home was a nightmare. After a delay due to the Airbus 'going tech' (broken) we were boarded onto a geriatric Russian Tupolev 154 that looked as if it hadn't flown for years. When the BA staff saw the plane they all crossed themselves, which didn't do much for my confidence, neither did the fact that the brakes stuck on and it took twenty minutes of full throttle engine revving to get moving. Eventually we got airborne, and I settled down in my loose lumpy seat, stared at the string luggage rack and thought of home. By the time the cabin crew had heated the food we were approaching Heathrow, but it did not matter, it was inedible. I thought, 'I hope air traffic control can speak Russian'. Eventually after a lot of banking and engine revving we landed amidst much clapping and cheering.

Gibraltar
With its low taxes and freedom of EC beaurocracy, Gibraltar makes an ideal base for both legitimate businesses and the laundering of the Spanish mafia. There are two very sticky problems that you can encounter, the many seagulls that crap on you and the apes that take delight in pooing on you. Seagull crap is white and runny while ape pooh is brown, smells vile and is a little more consistent. I write from experience. Japanese companies use Gibraltar as a doorway into Europe and the lucrative UN business for them has proved very useful to MMB. We supply many Toyota mobile clinics to the UN via a Gibraltar company. These are sometimes seen on newsreel shots from conflict areas like Afghanistan, Bosnia and Somalia.

Great Britain
Travelling around the United Kingdom does not make for exciting reading, however I remember one special incident. Flying from Manchester to Aberdeen via Dundee with a small airline proved that not all 'hairy' flights were confined to Africa. There were about 18 passengers on the Saab 340 jet and during the flight the pilot informed us that on arrival at Dundee he would first make a low level pass to frighten away the seagulls before landing -bird strikes are a major problem at Dundee. As we approached the weather conditions deteriorated rapidly, high winds and a full blizzard were throwing the small plane about like a discarded bag in a gale. All the passengers were very nervous and some were being sick when the pilot's reassuring voice came over the PA. He calmly announced that there was no danger of a bird strike as seagulls would not fly in these atrocious conditions.

The Highlands of Nigeria

My £30 visa

CHAPTER XII
NIGERIA

I have no photographs to accompany this chapter, because while things may be a little more relaxed now, at the time I visited Nigeria to display a camera in public was an invitation to be arrested. In spite of vast oil fields, the national currency, the Naira, was worth very little outside Nigeria and the US dollar was the currency of commerce. Most hotels and airlines would only accept dollars and even 'commissions' were normally paid in dollars although sterling is still acceptable if paid into an overseas bank account. There is nothing improper or illegal about the payments of commissions, they are your agent's legitimate fees and 'expenses'. Only the percentages are subject to scrutiny - it is wise not to ask how commission payments are arrived at.

To export to Nigeria a good agent is essential. He must have a detailed knowledge of your product and the potential customers - in my case the emergency services. His 'friends' and contacts should extend into government departments, customs, immigration, the federal bank and all the 'independent' vetting and inspection agencies whose purpose is to prevent corruption. A bank account in America, London, Switzerland, as well as Nigeria is essential. What we might view as corruption was an accepted part of everyday life in Nigeria and was regarded as a perk of most professional jobs. (I am not saying that any of my contracts or that any of the agents or officials I dealt with were anything less than transparently legitimate). With wealth and widespread poverty, crime was rife with kidnappings and robbery commonplace. Nigeria could be a very dangerous place for the western traveller.

MMB had an excellent agent who is still very active, and for this reason we will know him as Mr X. A likeable family man he sent his sons to the best private schools in England, and on to university, and he is highly respected in Nigeria and now a member of the government.

Like most English businessmen wishing to travel to Nigeria my ordeal began at the Nigerian High Commission visa office in London. I arrived early to find a disorderly queue several hundred yards long. The average wait was five hours and many would have to come back the following day. As instructed I ignored the queue and fought my way into the office shouting to the protesters that I was making a delivery. I could not reach the processing window for a sea of bodies all shouting and waving their applications and passports, I shouted out that I had come to see Abdul -- --. Again as briefed, immediately a side door opened and I was ushered inside.

The man at the desk presumably Abdul—— shook my hand. 'Good morning, Mr Hibbert, I am sorry about the mob rule out there,' he said in perfect English. On his desk was my pre-submitted application; I handed over my passport along with the legal £30 processing fee, and it was immediately stamped with my visa. The process had taken less than ten minutes and no 'incentives' changed hands, from his office in Lagos Mr X had done his job well, wheels had been oiled. I felt sorry for the hundreds queuing; they would have to wait many hours and sometimes days and for many their visa applications would be rejected without explanation.

As part of an ongoing contract it would be necessary to commission ambulances in the presence of a Minister of Health for a certain state, so I would depart for Nigeria the following week. Feeling somewhat apprehensive I boarded the British Airways, Heathrow to Lagos flight and settled down in the comfort of the club class cabin with the knowledge that our agent's office manager would meet me off the plane.

We landed at Lagos International airport in the very early hours of the morning (why can't long haul flights arrive at a civilised time?) in humid sweltering heat. Being club class my luggage had a priority label, so I should not have long to wait, I thought! Forty-five minutes at the immigration desk was followed by another two hours by the carousel before any luggage appeared. I was very tired and soaked with sweat and I was certainly not thinking straight. Just as I reached for my case a man in Nigerian national dress appeared at my side holding a piece of cardboard with the words 'MR HIBBERT'. Greatly relieved I foolishly blurted, 'Has Mr X sent you?' 'Yes' was the reply, 'I have a car outside, I will help you through customs'. I was impressed; our agent must have a lot of influence to get his man into this area. With a cursory nod to a customs officer, my 'escort' and I went straight through, passing the long queue and out into the arrivals hall.

With hundreds of 'meeters and greeters' it was absolute bedlam, as we fought our way through the crowd among the many name boards something caught my eye - was I imagining things or did I see another board for a MR HIBBERT? By now my escort was getting agitated with the crowd and by now I could clearly see the other board over the heads of the, it read 'MR HIBBERT MMB/XX (Mr Xs company). At this point alarm bells rang load and clear in my head, but my 'escort' had not seen the other board, and as we got close I waved an MMB ambulance brochure at the two men holding the board, at which they wrestled my case from the bogus escort and gave him a good kicking. I had had a very lucky escape; I would have been robbed and dumped in the back streets of a very dangerous city in the middle of the night with no money, luggage or passport. Having travelled in Africa previously I should have known not to tell the man who would be meeting me. The practice of buying names of airline passengers from baggage handlers and customs officers was commonplace and just one of the thousands of scams in Nigeria. But my ordeals had only just begun .

My new escorts, Mr X's manager and his driver took me to the Sheraton Hotel where after a beer and a bath I went to bed reflecting on what might have been. Next morning we set off for our agent's office in Lagos. Lagos has the world's worst traffic jams, even worse than Bangkok. At junctions and roundabouts, cars on the outside lanes are literally pushed to one side by lorries and buses resulting in damaged wings and wheels and more chaos. The short journey to the office took nearly two hours with some roundabouts taking twenty minutes to negotiate. Police roadside checks were everywhere, each one involving detailed explanations and so called document checks. Another problem was the piles of rubbish, rags and cardboard on the sides of the road, and when we were stopped alongside these, often a filthy and diseased hand would emerge hoping for a coin. Many of these 'bundles' would be run over and unceremoniously collected in pick up trucks 'dead or alive'. Do not visit Nigeria if the sight of poverty upsets you.

Part of my itinerary would take me to the Nigerian highlands; boarding the Katoka airlines old DC10 was reminiscent of Tanzania with a mad scramble on the airport tarmac even before the aircraft had stopped, followed by a 'push and shove' battle up the aircraft steps. The flight was made in an horrendous thunderstorm with lightning bouncing off the wings. We landed in torrential rain and appalling visibility without the aid of runway lights. The pilot must have been very good I thought; unfortunately he was killed a few weeks later along with 22 passengers when the plane crashed in similar conditions.

They had a British club that served delicious chips with the beer, and being high above sea level it meant a much cooler pleasant climate. In the just post-war years this was the Harrogate of Nigeria, with many wealthy Nigerians and white expatriates having luxurious second homes. I stayed at a hotel which had clearly seen better days. On the second night there was a knock at the door of my room, a roundhouse in the hotel grounds, and a young boy informed me that Mr X wanted to meet me urgently in Kano, a town about 200 miles to the north and that there was a taxi outside the hotel waiting for me. Having left Xs home only an hour earlier this was obviously a lie. I told the boy I would meet him in 30 minutes and I went immediately to reception and asked to look at the booking register. It showed my name and who had booked the room - in Nigeria this information is much sought after by criminals. I wiped the floor with the manager and was immediately moved into a suite in the main building, another kidnap attempt aborted, needless to say the youth and his accomplice did not come back.

Following the successful presentation the return flight to Lagos was with Nigerian Airways; the very old Boeing 737 was in a terrible state, the seats torn and loose, none of the overhead locker doors would remain closed, and the cabin crew had great difficulty in closing the cabin doors due to loose seals. I was sure I could see rivets vibrating in the wings.

Another two days were spent in the sultry heat and traffic jams of Lagos before my flight home. I couldn't wait! Having taken my luggage to the BA desk during the day Mr X was due to collect me from the hotel at 8pm for the 11.30pm flight to London. By 9pm he had not arrived, presumably trapped in the traffic jams! I was getting very worried, you just do not take a taxi after dark - even during the day all taxis in and out of the hotel are logged for security, but this service stops at night. By now I had no choice - I either miss the flight or risk a taxi. I called the guy lurking outside the hotel and asked for a taxi. 'How much to the airport?' '40 Naira and 10 Naira for my man' the driver replied. Reluctantly I got into the battered Datsun for the twenty minute journey and as we neared the airport I began to relax and make conversation with the driver. We turned away from the departure terminal. 'This is not the way' I said very forcibly. 'This is way for local flights' he replied (but there are no local flights at night). 'I want the international terminal.' 'That is 100 Naira' was the reply. '50', '90', '80', '70'. Done! Five minutes later as we drew up in front of the international terminal, I felt relieved.

At the airport I was surrounded by dozens of young boys all wanting to carry my brief case which I had no intention of parting with. Mr X had checked in my luggage earlier in the day. First stop the BA check in desk, no problems here. Second stop the airport departure tax kiosk. I handed over my passport to the overdressed female clerk along with the 100 Naira tax. It was immediately stamped and pushed to one side. 'You have present for poor girl, many dollars?' And her armed police minder glared at me. 'No dollars' I replied. 'No present, no passport,' she replied. The armed guard continued to stare. After a ten-minute confrontation I parted with 50 Naira, I had got off lightly, these people knew that travellers would willingly part with their cash, and Naira notes were no good outside Nigeria. This performance was repeated another five times before the departure lounge, at customs, security, special security, police checks, and even more so called security, by this time I had got rid of all my surplus Naira and thirty US dollars.

One more final hurdle before boarding was to identify your luggage on the tarmac and to sign for the benefit of British Airways that it was in good condition, nearly everyone's cases had been looted but no one objected. I couldn't wait to get out of this place (ironically within twelve months all the major airports in Nigeria would have an MMB ambulance). As soon as we boarded ice cold orange juice was served, never had a drink been more welcome. The BA cabin crew were well aware of the ordeal their passengers had to endure. I often heard passengers clap on landing but never before on take off, and when the pilot announced we had cleared Nigerian air space a great cheer went up, and during the next few hours I was to get extremely 'mellow' as the champagne flowed freely.

Six months on, following a series of crashes involving Nigerian Airways aircraft, the CAA banned all their flights over UK airspace, in turn the Nigerians banned all British flights. This led to a breakdown in political relations a situation that was to last for two years.

Today things have improved in Nigeria and you are no longer robbed at the airports, however Nigeria remains the scam capital of the world and even as I write the news is of a British engineer being kidnapped in the north of the country. The Queen is to visit the capital Abuja next week to open the Commonwealth conference. I sincerely hope that when she gets off the royal flight there is not a man on the tarmac holding a piece of cardboard with the words HM THE QUEEN. If so and she asks him if the President sent him he will surely reply 'Yes mom, I have a car waiting and will help you through customs.'

CHAPTER XIII
CABBAGES AND CONDOMS

THAILAND

Cabbages and Condoms is one of the worlds finest restaurants, situated in the centre of Bangkok, and it is next door to the 'Non-scalpel vasectomy centre' across the road from MacDonalds. It has a beautiful garden where all the trees and flowers are made from or adorned with multi-coloured condoms, in the souvenir shop you can buy a huge range of goods including imitation flowers all made from condoms. I have visited the restaurant but hasten to add not the vasectomy centre; the food is excellent with jumbo curried prawns the size of cod loins a specialty.

This is Thailand where at Bangkok airport the plane taxied through a golf course to get to its stand, and where the heat and humidity hits you like a sledgehammer when the doors are opened. The problem is getting into Bangkok which along with Lagos must have the world's worst traffic jams, and when leaving I must remember in addition to the three hours booking in time (now two at the new airport) to allow three hours to do the twenty minute journey to the airport.

There are two 'Hilton Hotels' in Bangkok, the Bangkok Hilton is the name given to the infamous prison where, if you are caught bringing anything more potent than an aspirin tablet into the country, you are incarcerated while awaiting the mandatory death penalty. When flying to Thailand never ever lose sight of your hand luggage, there is always a drug smuggler waiting to slip in a baggage. Thai police do not accept excuses, if you are caught you are dead, or if very lucky you will spend the rest of your life, twenty to a small cell in the Bangkok 'Hilton'

The Hilton Bangkok on the other hand is a beautiful hotel where one evening I was befriended by a rather large black American, we spent some time chatting, he insisted on having the drinks put on his bill. It wasn't until I joined the rest of the group that I discovered that my new found friend was the film actor Danny Glover.

My first visit to Thailand was made with a trade mission to promote our ambulances in association with the Thai LDV agent. Sponsored by the

British Government we organised and manned a stand at a medical and health product exhibition hosted by the British Ambassador and supported by the Duke and Duchess of Kent.

Manning an exhibition stand for five days is not the way most people would chose to spend their time in Bangkok; I did not get to see much of the cultural side of the city. However I did see a little more 'culture' at night. Sex is a huge industry in Thailand attracting tourists from all over the world. I thought I had 'seen it all' until I strolled the streets of Bangkok after dark; the thousands of bars and clubs offered mind-boggling services and entertainment - I will not go into detail.

The exhibition closed on the Friday with an evening reception at the nearby British Embassy hosted by the ambassador with the Duke and Duchess as guests of honour. I went along with my gold printed invitation in the company of two Yorkshire blokes, with the intention of making a speedy exit to a club as these receptions can often turn out to be very dull. The buffet was excellent but the wine was disappointing and to our horror the pre-poured glasses of whisky were watered down, obviously the Embassy head of finance was tight-arsed.

This serious situation had to be remedied; we cornered a very smart Gurkha sergeant, who looked like he would have been much happier shooting terrorists in the jungle than on Embassy attachment. He was obviously out of his depth, but explaining that we were representatives of the Scottish whisky industry, we asked 'was there no whisky straight from the bottle? With a 'just one moment sir, I will see what I can do,' he disappeared, emerging five minutes later with a bottle of 15-year-old Glenmorangie. 'Would this be all right sir, it's from the ambassador's apartment.' Our eyes lit up as we confirmed it would be fine. 'I will just check with his excellency,' said the sergeant. He stood no chance! In spite of his military training he was not fast enough, he was relieved of the bottle as we explained that the ambassador would be pleased to know that his guests were being so well looked after. Hiding the bottle behind a curtain away from prying eyes I vaguely remember that we had a very pleasant evening.

Cabbages & Condoms has since moved to the beautiful beach resort of Pattaya where it is now a world famous, first class holiday hotel and restaurant complex.

JORDAN

My sales visit to Jordan was made in the company of Nick Youdon, our object to visit our agents, the infamous Nero Brothers, who at the time were extremely successful at securing government contracts. Ali Nero, the oldest brother, could best be described as 'well-known well-connected and well - travelled'. There was always a loaded revolver in his desk draw and I remember one lunchtime how while cutting up a chicken with a dagger, he boasted that he had ways of dealing with anyone who crossed him. There was no mistaking his gestures.

Ali was well-known for his generous entertainment and would invite his guests to a night club, the drinks were always free and exotic dances would be performed at the table. And as the evening wore on and the drink loosened inhibitions, the dancers would sit on your knee and caress you. There was always a photographer on hand to ensure you had a memento to take home and that he had a 'record' of your evening's entertainment. If you fell for the dancers charms you would almost certainly take something home and it would not be a photograph.

Not to accept the invitation to go out with Ali would cause offence and as we were here to do business we had little choice but to accept. Nick and I were apprehensive when Ali collected us from the Intercontinental Hotel in his Range Rover to take us out for the evening. He drove like a maniac, and we were nervous wrecks by the time we arrived at the venue. We had a traditional Jordanian meal but both of us were keeping strictly to Perrier water. Ali ordered a whisky; a litre bottle of J&B was put on the table along with an attractive girl who made sure that Ali's glass was never empty.

With the whisky bottle nearly empty it was time for us to escape, so I doubled up clutching my stomach and moaned in pain. Nick confirmed I had been feeling ill all day and that we would have to return immediately to the hotel for my medication. Ali said he would take us straight away - Nick and I both looked at the empty whisky bottle, 'No we can not spoil your evening, will get a taxi' we said in unison, and quite an argument followed before we managed to convince Ali to stay with the girl. As soon as we arrived back at the hotel it was straight to the bar to celebrate our escape and drink to my acting ability, but next morning I had a terrible stomach ache - the food at the nightclub was definitely suspect.

Firing the Noonday Gun.

Causeway Bay, Hong Kong Island.

CHAPTER XIV
HONG KONG & THE NOONDAY GUN

Where else in the world could your wife take you shopping in Marks & Spencers at ten o'clock at night on Christmas day? Welcome to Hong Kong the city that never sleeps, where the Christmas lights are absolutely stunning and the shops will still be crowded at three o'clock in the morning.

Back in England on Christmas Day every town and village is deserted, not in Hong Kong, the streets, shopping malls and restaurants are not just crowded they are 'heaving'. This is a twenty-four hour a day buzzing city. The Chinese 'live to eat' and have something like 14,000 restaurants of every conceivable nationality to choose from. I have dined on drunken prawns and Peking crispy duck on a Sunday, the finest New Zealand fillet steak on Monday, dim-sum on Tuesday and in complete contrast then enjoyed North Sea cod, chips, mushy peas and a pint of Boddingtons at Harry Ramsden's where you can even buy take-away fish and chips wrapped in specially produced grease proof newspapers.

With a five night break in a luxury hotel costing less than some Spanish holidays, to travel to Hong Kong is very affordable, and around 2500 people arrive daily from the UK alone and processed at the airport with incredible efficiency. Hong Kong consists of 260 islands and covers 424 square miles; it is the most densely populated city in the world yet it is not difficult to find a beautiful deserted sandy beach. Now an SAR (Special Administration Region) of the People's Republic of China, it is no less exciting than it was before the hand over and is still a shopper's paradise.

What isn't quite so exciting now is the flight, today you land at Chep Lap Kok airport on Landau Island which is connected to the mainland by the world's longest road-rail suspension bridge. Chep Lap Kok is the most modern, futuristic and efficient airport in the world, it was also the most expensive and largest engineering project the world has ever seen. Built entirely on land reclaimed from the sea, two mountains were literally demolished to provide the rock, at one stage nearly all the dredgers in the world and the majority of the world's finest engineers were engaged on its construction.

However all my many visits to Hong Kong involved landing at the older and much more exciting Thai Kak airport, sandwiched between the peaks of Hong Kong Island and Kowloon, it was literally a piece of concrete sticking out into the bay with high rise flats on each side, and the runway for one of the busiest airports in the world.

Recognised by pilots as one of the most difficult airports in the world to land at, the approach involved banking in a tight turn to line up between the high rise buildings of Kowloon and the mountain peak of Hong Kong Island. I do not exaggerate when I say you could look out of the window when landing and see the occupants of the high rise flats enjoying their Kellogg's and noodles for breakfast. With long haul flights arriving from early morning local residents were used to seeing a jumbo jet pass their windows every three minutes and would often wave. For a plane to slide off the runway into the sea during the typhoon season was not uncommon.

All the Hong Kong statistics are mind boggling: there are more people per square mile than anywhere else in the world, more hotels classified as the 'world's finest', more Rolls Royces per square mile and even more millionaires than Alderley Edge. The amount of money gambled at one horse race meeting is staggering - more than is waged on the UK tote in a whole year - the tax alone raised at one meeting pays for the Hong Kong police force for the year.

In 1904 a Birmingham company built the Hong Kong tramways, and the colourful, uncomfortable double deck trams built on the old Glasgow style still run carrying literally over 100,000 passengers a day, the standard one dollar fare is thrown into a box when getting off, there are no tickets issued. In complete contrast the underground MTR (mass transit railway) is clean, efficient and safe and carries over a million passengers a day in long 'straight through' British-built Metro Camel coaches. Elsie and I have used the MTR in the early hours of the morning, the trains, subways and stations were as always, spotlessly clean and crowded with a mix of white and Chinese. At 3am passengers from every corner of the globe mingled together in perfect safety, smartly dressed couples in evening dress would be heading home or to their hotels after a concert or night club visit, sitting side by side with the local population going to work.

If you haven't been on the Star Ferry you haven't been to Hong Kong. The famous green ferries cost one HK dollar (about 8p) and cross Victoria Harbour, the world's busiest shipping lane. The ferries depart every few minutes, 24 hours a day from the Ocean Ferry terminal in Kowloon, which is adjacent to the huge Ocean Centre shopping mall. The crossing to the Star ferry terminal at Central on Hong Kong Island takes 15 minutes; it is absolutely incredible how the ferries manage not to collide with all the other shipping ranging in size from cruise liners to junks, plus the many high speed hydrofoils speeding to and from Macau.

Most of my many visits to Hong Kong have been with Cathay Pacific but I have also flown with BA, Emirates and even on a geriatric British Caledonian 747. I soon got into a routine to help combat jet lag. After leaving the UK for the 15 hour flight it would be around 10.30am when I would check into my favourite hotel, the Excelsior on Causeway Bay. After a coffee and a shower I would take the tram to Central, and then the mountain tramway to the Peak. After savouring the awe-inspiring views I would then make the two hour walk around the Peak then down through the woods back

Po-Lin Monastery

to Central and make straight for the 'Bull and Bear'. By this time I would be very hot, tired and thirsty. At the Bull and Bear, homemade steak and kidney pie would be washed down with ice cold lager. It was then on to the MTR for the high speed five minute journey back to Causeway Bay and the Excelsior. It would now be about 3.30pm, a long soak, followed by six hours sleep and I was ready for a few English draught beers and some late night entertainment in the Dickens Bar, before going to bed about 2.00am, waking refreshed ready for the day's business meetings.

The next few days would be dedicated to business, first a meeting with our agents and now personal friends, Jimmy Chu and Kenrick Ho, who used to work for Jardine Engineering Ltd, but now own their own company. There would be visits to the Chief Ambulance Officer at Fire Brigade HQ, various government departments and agencies, franchised motor dealers, the Royal Hong Kong Jockey Club (we supplied them with ambulances) and many more. Meetings would often involve lunch, always at a top restaurant. I loved every minute of it. Hong Kong hospitality is not only legendary it is I believe the most professional in the world. During one visit Elsie and I had Jardine's luxury junk at our disposal on Boxing Day, along with Jimmy, Kenrick, and their girlfriends we went on an island cruise in beautiful sunshine.

I could spend a long time writing about Hong Kong and my love for it but there are four special events that I need to tell you about: 'Going to the races' at Happy Valley, a visit to Po-Lin monastery, Kenrick's wedding and what was one of the proudest moments of my life, firing the Noonday Gun.

During a visit to Po-Lin monastery on Landau island you witness two events what must surely be the 'ultimate' in the old world meeting the new. The gold Buddha at Po-Lin is the second largest in the world, but inside the gold plated head and body it is air conditioned. The huge tree trunk that swings to strike the gigantic bell to summon the monks to prayer was brought in from China, it looks and is incredibly ancient - but the complicated mechanism is computer controlled.

In the monastery garden I watched monks from a distance doing penance in complete silence, but while busily hoeing the vegetable plot one monk looked furtively around to see if any of his superiors were around before lifting up his habit, 'The poor lad's bursting and is going to have a pee,' I thought. Nothing of the sort, from under his rope he extracted a mobile phone and started chattering away in Cantonese, presumably to a fellow monk in China.

If caught perhaps he would have been on bread and water for six months.

In May 1997 Elsie and I received an unexpected wedding invitation from Kenrick and his fiancée Lilian. Hong Kong was a long way to travel for a wedding but we had no hesitation in accepting, the wedding was to be ten days before the hand-over to China and at this time Hong Kong was facing a very uncertain future.

On the morning of the wedding Kenrick's family went through the Chinese custom of kidnapping the bride from her parent's home. There was lots of mock fighting to defend the bride's honour before the families unite, a (prearranged) dowry is agreed and the wedding now proceeds amid much celebration. The first stage of the proceedings was the legal civil ceremony at the Tsim Sha Tsui Cultural Centre which is close to the Star Ferry terminal. This was conducted in accordance with British law, however in ten days time with Chinese rule this would all change. It is noticeable now that all the royal coats of arms have already been removed from inside and the outside of civic buildings, outside even the post boxes have had their coats of arms ground off.

In the evening there was a wedding dinner in the Crystal Ballroom at the Holiday Inn in Nathan Road. The banquet started with suckling pig followed by fourteen other courses. I'm ashamed to say that Elsie let me down by asking for a knife and fork while I persevered with chopsticks. It was a wonderful evening with lots of fun, games and laughter. There was no loud music and no one was the worse for drink. During the evening Lilian changed dresses three times, first she wore a western style wedding dress, followed by a beautiful ball gown and finally to say goodbye to all the guests she wore a traditional Chinese kimono. Both sets of parents visited every table with a large glass and a bottle of VSOP brandy to wish every guest good luck. The glass was raised but the brandy never touched. And at the end of the evening, in accordance with Chinese tradition, instead of a piece of wedding cake all the guests received a portion of suckling pig in a special 'take away' box.

This was to be my last visit to Hong Kong before retiring and it was a truly memorable visit that started with a personal tour of HMS Chatham the British naval frigate that would escort the Royal Yacht Britannia back to Britain with Chris Patten the last governor of Honk Kong. Kirk Leach a member of the crew and a Bollington lad who we knew well showed us all over the ship. We were surprised to see how many girls there were among the crew - what a tale we had to tell Kirks parents when we got home.

THE NOONDAY GUN

'Mad dogs and Englishmen
Go out it the midday sun,
In Hong Kong they strike a gong,
And fire off a Noonday gun.'

The immortal words of Noel Coward's famous song, the Noonday gun is a legend in part surrounded by mystery. It is part of Hong Kong's history and now a major tourist attraction. The gun is fired 366 time a year and it was feared that when the Chinese took over in 1997 it would be banished. However after extensive negotiations the Chinese authorities realised its value to tourism and have allowed the tradition to continue.

It is situated in a lovely raised plot surrounded by ornate railings on the Causeway Bay promenade close to the Royal Hong Kong Yacht Club - the RHKY refused to bow to Chinese pressure and was the only HK club allowed to keep its royal title. Others such as the Jockey club and the Golf club were stripped of their titles. The Noonday Gun is one of those locations that can be clearly seen from everywhere but is difficult to find your way to. There is a walkway tunnel from the Excelsior hotel car park that goes under the busy dual carriageway that skirts the bay, coming out on the promenade close to the gun. It is little used but is lit and is safe. The only other access is by a footbridge from nearby Victoria Park, and this route is worth taking if only to see the locals taking their birds for a walk (in their cages). It also is a place to practice Tai Chi.

The Noonday Gun belongs to Jardine's (now Jardine Matheson) and it is on land sold at public auction in 1891 and still officially registered as plot number one. The plot, bought for a few dollars, is now one of the most valuable pieces of real estate in the world, and houses the Excelsior Hotel, Caesar's Palace restaurant, the world trade centre and various office blocks.

Jardines was a trading company founded in Canton in 1832, and the 'boss' was known as the Tai Pan. Whenever the Tai Pan sailed into the bay in his fast clipper laden with goods the cannon was fired to signal his arrival, as a salute and a signal to let the workers know that the 'boss' had arrived. One day the Tai Pan arrived in his schooner and was making a good rate of knots just off East Point, when ahead of it was one of Her Majesty's ships with the admiral on board. The Tai Pan's schooner was faster and just as it was overtaking the cannon was fired. To pass one of her Majesty's ships was bad enough but to fire a gun was an insult. The admiral when ballistic.

Jardines senior personnel were summoned to Government House to explain on whose authority the cannon was fired; of course they had no authority but had no reason to think they needed any. As punishment they were ordered to cease the practice forthwith and to fire the cannon every day on the stroke of noon as a time signal for Hong Kong. This practice has continued ever since with the exception of the Japanese occupation in World War II. The original cannon, an old naval gun, disappeared during the occupation, but after the war in 1946 the Royal Navy unearthed a suitable replacement from the dockyard and presented it to Jardines. This gun is still in use today, a Hotchkiss Mark 1 three pounder naval gun made in England in 1900 and which served on HMS Southampton and took part in the battle of Jutland in1916. It then saw further service on board HMS Cardiff during the Second World War and is a tribute to British engineering.

The gun is fired every day at noon by an immaculately uniformed Jardine employee known as the 'Guard' in a ceremony watched and photographed by tourists from all over the world. Just before noon a polished brass shell is placed in the gun breach by the guard, and carefully checking his watch he rings six bells on a ship's bell before pulling the firing cord. An ear shattering bang rings out across Victoria Harbour followed by a plume of white smoke, eight bells are then rung 'to summon the forenoon watch'.

The tourists who have been busy with their cameras are then allowed into the site to have their pictures taken alongside the gun.

VIPs are sometimes invited to perform the firing ceremony, visitors such as Royalty, politicians, presidents, ambassadors and governors. On the list of people who have fired the gun is Noel Coward and the last governor of Hong Kong Chris Patten. Also on the list is one Graham G Hibbert.

It is considered a great honour and recognition of successful business achievements for a department of Jardines (they employ 200,000 people) to be allocated a guest firing, when this honour fell to the CED department of Jardine Engineering Ltd, I was their chosen guest and I felt very privileged.

On the day, many of the department's employees and their families turned out for the ceremony. I was allowed to bring one guest so I took along a very nice Yorkshire lass from Bradford called Fiona Ellison, who was leading a West Yorkshire trade mission to Hong Kong. Now Fiona had a wicked sense of humour and as we gathered around the gun she nearly brought chaos to the proceedings. Following a briefing by Jardine's PR lady and a short rehearsal there followed a few minutes wait for the time signal. By now a sizable crowd of tourists had gathered, mostly Americans and Japanese. I was stood by the gun nervously holding the cord when Fiona walked to the bottom of the steps and performed a perfectly executed curtsy to me. Over the traffic noise I could hear the buzz of excitement from the onlookers, there was much pushing and shoving as they jostled for the best positions and I remember looking up to a sea of cameras.

At five seconds before midday the Guard rang the bell four times, paused then rang two more, 'BANG', I am pleased to say that it went to plan and I didn't pull the cord to soon. When they opened up to admit the public the poor PR lady was inundated by tourists wishing to know who the important royal visitor was. An American gentleman asked if he could shake my hand and asked Fiona who I was. 'Sorry, security,' she said. 'I understand' said the American, and his very loud wife shouted, 'Oh my gawd, I can't wait to get home to tell the grand-kids.' I tried desperately to keep my face straight while Japanese tourists had their photographs taken with me during my moment of fame.

When we eventually escaped, the whole party retired across the road to Caesar's Palace for a magnificent Chinese banquet starting with, you've guessed it, Peking crispy duck, drunken prawns and pancakes.

You may recollect I said that the Noonday Gun was fired 366 times a year (367 in leap years), on New Years Eve large crowds gather on Causeway Bay where all the trees are decorated with thousands of white fairy lights, they are entertained by the pipes and drums of the Hong Kong police band, everyone dances Scottish reels, and shortly before midnight a Scottish piper leads a procession to the gun which is fired on the stroke of midnight, always by a lady, to signal in the New Year.

As Auld Lang Syne is sung the night sky is illuminated by a gigantic firework display, dancing and merriment continue into the wee small hours - when if you have any energy left you can still go shopping.

Hong Kong is a wonderful place to spend Christmas.

CHAPTER XV
BUCKINGHAM PALACE

Brigadier John Davies is one of England's true gentlemen, charming, impeccable manners and a personal friend of the late Queen Mother and Princess Diana. He was the perfect choice as chairman of the Commonwealth Society for the Deaf with responsibility for fund raising. John came up with the name Sound Seekers and launched the HARK! project. He was instrumental in persuading Prince Andrew to take over as patron on the death of Princess Diana and recruiting Sir Trevor MacDonald as the society's president. Sound Seekers look after deaf children and educate staff in the treatment of audio related conditions in the third world.

Enter MMB. John Davies contacted us to see if his dream of a small but versatile mobile clinic capable of penetrating into the African bush could become reality. I was soon on my way to London and as a result of the initial meeting the seeds for the HARK! mobile clinics were soon to grow and bear fruit. Based on the Land Rover Defender 130 chassis the first HARK! was allocated to Uganda. John had a remarkable ability to raise money and at a champagne reception held in a Mayfair showroom I ceremoniously handed the keys of the first HARK! to the Ugandan High Commissioner. Present at the ceremony were the Secretary of the Commonwealth, many high

commissioners and ambassadors, Sir Trevor MacDonald, showbiz personalities, company executives and the press.

I should add that the prestigious venue which would have normally cost thousands of pounds was provided free of charge as were all the drinks and a five star buffet. Such was John's fundraising ability that the President of Fyffe's Bananas promised to ship the first HARK! clinic to Uganda free of charge. In two hours enough money was pledged for a second HARK! which would be destined for the Western Cape of South Africa with the chief executive of South African Airways offering to fly it to Cape Town in a 747 freighter.

Six months later the second HARK! was completed and another high profile ceremony in London's Mayfair was held but this time with a difference - the hand over was to be at Buckingham Palace. These lavish ceremonies may seem extravagant but they were immensely important, they were a means of thanking the donors, a lot of money came from the States and Jersey for instance, and the publicity was invaluable in the constant battle to win the corporate sponsorship of international companies.

After the showroom 'bash', six invited VIPs, John, Trevor Macdonald and myself left for the short drive to Buckingham Palace. I drove the HARK! following the lead car down the Mall, sweeping around the Queen Victoria Memorial we slowed down in front of the Palace. After a brief word with the police, the gates swung open and we drove onto the forecourt past the impeccable sentries and on into the inner courtyard.

Charlotte Manley, Prince Andrew's attractive private secretary came out to brief us on the formalities and details of the 'photo call'. We were all lined up in order of presentation to the Prince, with John doing the introductions. I thought all this a bit stuffy and formal but once the introductions were over the atmosphere changed with lots of laughing and joking.

For the benefit of the press I formally handed over the keys to Prince Andrew, the keys were actually my car and house keys and we joked about him not being able to keep them. Andrew was brilliant, he had done his homework, and he knew a lot about Macclesfield Motor Bodies (MMB) and asked lots of technical questions about the manufacture of the clinic. I found him an extremely nice person with an infectious laugh but I must admit it was with a tinge of sadness that the thought went through my mind, 'had not Princess Diana been killed this presentation would have been with her'.

I was very proud and honoured to meet Prince Andrew - thousands of

people have the honour of been introduced to royalty but very few get to chat with them in private and I never dreamed that this privilege would extend to Prince Andrew's Mother and that I would actually get to know his father well.

With all the logistical overheads, technical equipment and local staff training, the mobile clinic cost well over £100,000 for each HARK! Project, Five have been completed in different parts of the Commonwealth and there are others planned. Thanks to Sound Seekers, John Davies's dedication and the MMB mobile clinics, many deaf children in the third world can now hear.

Media personalities like to be associated with charities for personal reasons and of course it is also good for their image. Supplying medical vehicles to international charities and disaster relief organisations brought me into contact with many including John Snow, Sir Trevor MacDonald, Stuart Hall, Terry Waite, Felicity Goodie, Anita Roddick, the Secretary of the Commonwealth, members of the royal family, many ambassadors and high commissioners, tribal chiefs and sheikhs.

Two years before the Hark! projects Elsie and I were invited to the BBC studios in London to meet Esther Ransen at a recording of 'That's Life' in which an MMB ambulance was donated to a children's hospital in St Petersburg. A few weeks later the ambulance was shown on national TV on life saving emergencies on the streets of St Petersburg.

CHAPTER XVI
SANDRINGHAM & BALMORAL

In order to promote British products overseas the DTI (Department for Trade & Industry) sponsor trade fairs, seminars and trade missions where members of the royal family and other VIPs are used to promote British goods. These 'all expenses paid jollies' are popular, normally include wives and would nearly always include a cocktail party in the presence of an 'HRH' at the British embassy or high commission by invitation of the ambassador.

I went to many of these functions and met among others HRH The Duke and Duchess of Kent and HRH The Duke and Duchess of Gloucester, whom I found aloof but sincere and they did take their duties seriously. The same could not be said for Lord David Owen who I found arrogant and unsociable. At the United Nations World Aid exhibition in Geneva he spent more time on the Japanese stands instead of 'flying the British flag'. By far the most interesting and sincere man I met at these events was Terry Waite; we shared a bottle of red wine in Geneva and we got on 'like a house on fire'. After all he was born in Bollington where his father was village policeman for a time before moving to Styal. Little did I dream that ten years later Terry would hold my one year old grandson, Samuel, as he opened the Bollington discovery centre.

In Spring 2000 events were put in train that would lead me to visit the royal households at Sandringham and Balmoral, with private meetings for both Elsie and myself with The Queen and the Duke of Edinburgh.

Possibly as a result of my presentation of the Hark! clinics to the Duke of York at Buckingham Palace, MMB was commissioned by Prince Philip to design and build a customised 'off road' personnel carrier for use at Sandringham and Balmoral. It was to be built on a Land Rover Defender 130 chassis and a meeting was arranged at Sandringham to discuss the specification.

Present at the meeting was David Key the Duke's personal driver and 'right hand man'. David was a likable character from London's East End who had been with the Duke for many years. Land Rover was represented by their Royal Household liaison executive, George Hassel and my old friend Nick Youdon from the special vehicle division.

The initial meeting was held at the Sandringham House mews. The

Duke, now in his 79th year, arrived at speed on a motorbike not wearing a crash helmet (it is a private estate), and following the initial introductions by David Key - 'Good morning, sir' was the only formality - we all got down to business in a relaxed and informal manner with lots of laughing and joking. I had a preconceived idea that Prince Philip was stuffy, arrogant and difficult to get on with, instead as I would again find at Balmoral he was charming, good fun and a pleasure to work with.

One thing you learn on these occasions is that because you feel honoured to be doing work for the royal family it is very easy to lose sight of the financial aspect and agree to specification changes without taking account of the costs involved. I would not go as far as to say that the Royals exploit this but they are certainly not adverse to taking advantage of it. On more than one occasion I had to firmly point out to Prince Philip that he would have to dig deeper into the royal purse if he wanted a particular addition to the original specification.

Fourteen weeks later the chassis was delivered to Macclesfield and the production of the sixteen seat, dog carrying deluxe Land Rover commenced. I liased during the production stage through David Key. After a small hiccup over the exterior colour, the vehicle was completed in August and duly registered. Because it was a royal household vehicle it was not subject to Ministry of Transport type approval; it is also interesting to note that the registration number is not on the DVLC computer. When a photograph of the vehicle appeared in the newspapers in November, reporters and others who checked out the number would find that it did not exist - the vehicle like other royal cars is registered by a secret Government department in London.

Prince Philip requested that the hand over should take place during the Royal Family's annual holiday at Balmoral Castle, so Land Rover arranged the delivery details and a date was fixed in the first week of September. There was no way Elsie was going to let me go on my own this time; I contacted David Key who sought the approval of Prince Philip, and he readily agreed for her to accompany me. As this was to be a private visit he personally organised her security clearance with Scotland Yard's Royal protection department.

We stayed over night at the Glen Lui Hotel in Ballater which is where many of the special branch officers, drafted in when the Royal Family are in residence at Balmoral, stay. Ballater is a lovely little town. Royals can often be seen shopping there and nearly every shop including the newsagents, butchers, chemists and greengrocers proudly displays the Royal coat of arms.

The plan was to for David Key to collect George Hassel from Aberdeen airport and for us to meet at the castle entrance near to Crathy Church for the 10.30 appointment. However the Birmingham flight was over an hour late so Elsie and I had to go ahead At the Castle entrance a pleasant plain clothes policeman was expecting us and directed us through the castle grounds to the estate office and mews stables about four minutes walk from the castle.

As we got out of the car outside the mews, a small woman wearing a tweed jacket, immaculate brown jodhpurs and a silk headscarf on her head rode past us on a magnificent and well-groomed stallion. Elsie was ecstatic; 'It's the Queen, it's the Queen, I've seen the Queen close up'. She was absolutely thrilled; 'my friends are not going to believe this', she said.

I went into the office where refreshments were on offer, but as I came out of the office ten minutes later I was flabbergasted to find Elsie and the Queen chatting like long lost friends. They were completely on their own, no aids, police or staff to be seen. 'Your Highness, may I introduce my husband', Elsie said. I was nearly speechless. 'Good morning Ma'am'. We had been told that you address her as 'Ma'am' as in 'Jam'! and not 'Marm' as in 'Jarm'). Elsie noticed she wore only a wedding ring and a beautiful engagement ring.

The Queen knew why we there and told us, 'He's gone fishing; he knows you have arrived and should not be long'. She talked about the new vehicle and, no doubt well aware of her husbands 'hairy' driving, was concerned about its stability and off road handling. She knew that the Duke's new vehicle had been built in Cheshire and told us about the progress of her new Bentley in production at Crewe, to be completed in time for her forthcoming Golden Jubilee. We talked about our families and she was pleased that I had met Prince Andrew. I realised the Queen was enjoying this relaxed 'chat' in complete privacy - there was no hint of a 'plum in the mouth' or formality. We said our goodbyes and wished her well for her Jubilee. She left us to walk back to the Castle alone. What an experience and a tale to tell, very few people get to shake hands with The Queen and even less have the opportunity to talk with her in private. Elsie's face was radiant.

A few minutes late Prince Philip arrived on his motorbike - again helmetless - to be followed shortly after by David Key and George Hassel. I introduced Elsie. The new vehicle was now in front of the garage it would share with the Rolls Royces and Bentleys. The inspection commenced. The Duke was delighted and called his new toy Jumbo Three. 'Road test time', he said.

Elsie said 'I will wait in the car.' 'No Mrs Hibbert, you are coming in the cab with me, the others can sit in the back,' said the Duke. With her high heels and stiff knees Elsie had some difficulty in getting into the high cab, but no sooner was she in than we set off at a rate of knots through the castle grounds.

As we climbed up onto the moors I became somewhat concerned that a 79 year old man with a reputation for the ladies was chatting to my wife while driving at speed on dirt roads with hairpins and steep drops, in a vehicle he was not familiar with. I need not have worried, the Duke was an accomplished driver. During the forty minute drive the Duke and Elsie managed to talk about their families, the Queen Mum, Elsie's father and our children, Jane and Peter. He was the perfect gentleman and he gave her a running commentary about the Castle and the gardens. I wonder how many visitors to Balmoral Castle get the Duke of Edinburgh as their personal driver and guide?

We left for home on 'cloud nine'. The friendly royal protection officer was still on the gate and took our photograph for us at the entrance. My career was nearing an end - what a climax this had been and for Elsie too. I was so happy for her.

CHAPTER XVI
FINALE

All of the stories documented in this book have been about my working life, with the exception of this last chapter; this account is a little about a very special holiday, when Elsie and I decided to celebrate our 60th birthdays together with something we would always remember.

The plan was a ride on the Orient Express, a cruise around the Mediterranean on the Oriana, by coach from Monte Carlo to Nice and finally returning home on Concorde.

We met up with our fellow passengers at the special platform at Waterloo station to board the famous Orient Express to Southampton's ocean terminal. In fact the 'express' meandered through the Thames valley and the Hampshire countryside taking all morning to reach Southampton. In our beautifully restored Victorian coach a magnificent champagne lunch was served, and it was perhaps the result of the champagne and good wine that when we boarded the coach at Southampton docks for the short transfer to the Oriana, we discovered to our horror that we were heading into the New Forest with a party of Welsh landladies.

We were not alone; four other passengers had made the same mistake, but after the initial panic, we had a 'whip round' and with encouragement from the landladies the driver turned the coach around and headed at full speed for the cruise liner terminal. As we drew alongside the Oriana the landladies, who were enjoying every minute of the drama, let out a resounding cheer. The gang plank was literally pulled up behind us; we had made it with seconds to spare, minutes later as the bands played, the liner's powerful side thrusters started to push the huge vessel away from the quay as it set sail without the aid of tugs.

As we sailed down Southampton Water we passed what remains of Netley Hospital. I looked out with great emotion as I remembered 39 years earlier, as a national service man, watching from the hospital shore line the great liners sailing by, never imagining that one day I would be on one of them. Two of our friends from home, Marjorie and Lawrence Holt were sitting in the Netley country park waving at the Oriona as it passed - we were stood on the upper deck waving at the crowds but at the time we did not know they were there, nor did they know we were on board.

The great cruise liner lived up to its name, with wonderful food and entertainment. The Oriana is a 'one class' ship, and we mingled and drank with the many celebrities on board including Jimmy Saville, who we got to know quite well.

After several ports of call including Gibraltar that I knew so well, the final port was Monte Carlo where a coach was waiting to take us to Nice for a two hour stay before going on to the airport. In Nice we decided to forego the pleasure of paying about £17 for a cup of coffee and a dry ham roll but as usual I was bursting for a pee and had to search around for a 'hommes', eventually finding one on the promenade.

Unfortunately I hadn't any francs, and became embroiled in an altercation with an arrogant French toilet attendant who was handing out two tiny sheets of toilet paper in exchange for one franc (or five francs - no change was given). There was no way he was going to let an Englishman into his toilet without paying even though I didn't want any of his precious paper. I was becoming more desperate - I eventually sneaked in when he was arguing with another poor soul who had no francs.

When I came out feeling much better I was, along with the rest of the English race, verbally abused by the little Frenchman who then proceeded to chase me along the promenade demanding his franc. I rarely make gestures but this time one finger followed by two seemed essential - and I looked back to see the other chap in need dash into the loo. I never did like the French.

At Nice airport we had the use of the VIP lounge with its free wines and cognacs, and on the tarmac we were given time to look around Concorde and take photographs before boarding, into what at first impression, looked like the inside of a long drainpipe with seats. The cabin may be a bit on the narrow side but it is luxurious, and the grey leather seats are comfortable with lots of leg room. On each side of the partition bulkheads there is a screen displaying the speed and other flight details. The compact galley is in the middle of the passenger cabin.

Concorde takes off at 225 MPH, reaching this speed in just 30 seconds, the four Rolls Royce Olympus engines with after burners thrust it into the sky forcing you back into your seat. We settled down to a meal of smoked roast breast of duck, washed down with champagne, and throughout the flight the pilot gave an enthralling running commentary.

Concorde headed out over the Atlantic and soon reached the cruising altitude of 60,000 feet, the edge of space. When Mach 2 (twice the speed of sound) came up on the flight display a huge cheer rang out. At this point the captain invited all the passengers to visit the cockpit, two at a time, and squeeze, one at a time, into the cockpit to sit alongside the flight engineer, surrounded by literally hundreds of instruments. Looking forward through the cockpit window on the edge of space all you could see was very dark blue 'nothing'. There was no impression of travelling at 1600 miles per hour.

The champagne never stopped until we started to descend for landing at Heathrow. Unfortunately the New York Concorde flight had just landed and prevented us using the special Concorde terminal. It was with some difficulty after all the champagne that we slowly disembarked down the narrow steps. We caught the Virgin intercity train at Euston. The two hour journey back to Macclesfield in an overcrowded coach, with everyone competing to see who could talk the loudest on their mobile phones, was hell. What a come down! And I was thinking all the time, this trip would have taken just nine minutes on Concorde.